Durham Miners' Millennium Book

David Temple

Dedicated to the former mining communities of the County of Durham

ISBN 1 901237 18 4

Printed and published by TUPS Books, in association with the NUM Durham Area
30 Lime Street, Newcastle upon Tyne NE1 2PQ
Tel No: 0191 222 0299 Fax: 0191 233 0578

Preface

No working men have been more conscious of their history than miners and no union has contributed more to the struggle for rights than the miners' union. But often the details of this history are not widely known even in the mining communities. *The Durham Miners' Millennium Book* is an attempt to tell the story of our mining communities, a story which is as relevant today as it was at any time in the past, because it is a story of self-reliance. Miners did not wait for the welfare state to be created for them they created it around them with their co-op stores, their clinics, welfare halls, playing fields and clubs.

Central to their struggle was the fight to create a union which would protect them from the constant attacks of the owners and the government. Sometimes it appeared that miners suffered one defeat after another, and it is true that their were many setbacks and cruel disappointments. But when we look at the history as a whole, as this book does, we can see that the general movement was forwards, and this was a result of men and women refusing to quietly accept the dictates of those who were in authority over them.

Many miners who are now dispersed into other industries continue to fight for their rights in new circumstances. Durham communities may be the poorer for the loss of our industry but they still have a pride that is rooted in the past. For confirmation we have to look no further than the Durham Miners' Gala which continues to attract large crowds in celebration of the traditions which have sustained us over the years.

David Guy

President NUM Durham Area

Author's note

When I first began to plan this *Durham Miners' Millennium Book* I thought it would consist of a collection of articles on different aspects of coalfield life, around which I would write a historical narrative. When I actually got down to the writing I soon discovered that there was enough material for at least three books, and if I was to include many illustrations and photographs then the book would have to be limited to a historical narrative centred on the union, which in Durham dominated social and industrial life.

I would like to thank all those people who have provided me with written work and photographs. What I haven't included in this book will be included in a future book about coalfield culture and personalities and another dealing in detail with miners' memories of the 1984 / 85 strike and its aftermath.

No one who writes a book of this type starts from scratch but from a wealth of material published by others. I owe a debt of gratitude to many authors who have done us all a great service by chronicling a history of which the people of Durham are justly proud.

I would particularly like to thank those who helped with the research: my friend and comrade Cliff Slaughter for his work on the first half of the 20th century, Alistair Robinson for lending me his excellent thesis on the 1844 strike, Carol Roberton for her consistent help and support with photographs and material, James Tuck for his help in identifying photographs, Gerald R Ash, Albert H Cooper, James Kennedy, Keith Pattinson, Stan Gamester for the loan of photographs, and the agents and staff in the Miners Hall, Redhill for their support over many years and the access they gave me to photographic and documentary archives.

I would like to thank all those sponsors whose names are recorded at the back of this book who made this production possible. Finally I would like to thank all my 'marras' in the coal industry alongside whom I worked and fought for 21 years before the untimely demise of the coalfield. It is they who have inspired *The Durham Miners' Millennium Book.*

David Temple

Foreword

County Durham is synonymous with coal and it would be almost impossible to have been born in the county and not have any forbears or relatives who have not been involved with or owed their livelihood to coal or its related industries

This book tells the story of the Durham miners, their rich heritage and culture, collective unity and loyalty to their trade union. It is a history of struggle against oppression and tyranny from the beginning of coal extraction in the county of Durham until the closure of the last Durham pit, Wearmouth colliery, under the auspices of British Coal, formerly the NCB..

From the early years of mining our forefathers battled to establish collective protection through trade unionism. Many attempts to establish a union were ruthlessly put down by the capitalist coal owners including the Earls of Durham, Lord Londonderry and the Bishops of Durham. Miners were virtually owned by their 'masters' in a legal mechanism known as the yearly bond. Only when the bond was effectively smashed in a historic strike at Wearmouth colliery and subsequent court case in Sunderland was the union as we know it established in 1869. After the establishment of the union the struggle was by no means over. Miners had to battle not only against the owners but also the collaborationist policies of their leaders.

In 1921 and 1926 miners were locked in battle to protect wages and conditions. Miners endured the depression of the 1930s and won their greatest achievement when the mines were nationalised in 1947, the culmination of of over 50 years of agitation.

It was, however, not until the strikes of the 1970s that miners secured their largest wage rises. To do so, in 1974 they had to defeat a Tory government. Following this victory further advances were made in wage levels, health and safety, pensions and many other fringe benefits.

But the battle lines were drawn in the 1980s, culminating in the war of all wars to protect our jobs and communities. We were confronted by a government which detested everything miners and their communities stood for and used all its repressive forces in order to defeat us. This together with the power of the media led to the isolation of the miners in their struggle. Within a few years came pit closures on a massive scale, and the Durham coalfield perished.

This thoroughly interesting book chronicles the many industrial and political conflicts of a proud union and a great community of men and women.

David Hopper

General Secretary, NUM Durham Area

Index

Chapter 1

For the greater part of two millenniums the North East of England remained a remote, thinly populated dangerous place to live: a buffer zone between two warring nations.

The counties of Northumberland and Durham had such little economic importance that they did not warrant a mention in the Doomsday book. The inclement climate and barren uplands produced a poor living for lord and peasant alike. There were years of moderate prosperity but, just as the population began to grow and life became bearable, barbarous devastation ensued as raiding parties from the North ravaged the land.

In peacetime it was cowboy country. Its towns were trail towns. Nervous drovers from over the border slowly cajoled huge herds of highland cattle down over the Cheviot and Pennine hills southward and on to Smithfield.

The North East did have wealth, but the full extent of this fabulous wealth lay hidden well below the surface soil, trapped in the strata.

It is now well known that coal was used by the Romans when they built Hadrian's wall between 122 and 126 AD. Long sections of the wall were built along the steep sides of the Winsill, an outcrop of volcanic rock, which dominates the geology of the North East from Holy Island in the North to the lower valley of the Tees.

Historians speculate that when building the wall the Romans uncovered local outcrops of coal which they used to heat their baths.

However, coal was of little economic importance while England had an abundance of wood in the extensive oak and beech forests. The sweet smoke of wood fire was much preferred to the acrid, sulphurous fumes of fire coal. Why chase coal into its subterranean world when trees could be harvested so easily in the broad light of day?

The second millennium was three centuries old before coal began to have any importance to the English economy and it was, from the beginning, controversial.

In 1303 the freemen of Gateshead appealed to King Edward to intervene in their dispute with Bishop Bec, the Bishop of Durham, over the mining of ironstone and coal on their lands.

By 1306 the citizens of London were complaining of the noxious fumes from the coal-fuelled kilns and furnaces of smithies, brewers, dyers and lime-burners.

This was feudal Britain at a time when the vested interests of landowners took precedence over the innovation and enterprise of freemen and merchants. Monopoly and tax were economic weapons against the upstarts of the emerging middle classes. In Durham the largest and most powerful of these feudal landowners were the Prince Bishops, who were keen to profit from the exploitation of coal but were equally careful to restrict and control the trade. Early leases were expensive to acquire and riddled with conditions and restrictions which inhibited extensive operations.

In 1303 Thomas Gray, a Knight, and John Pulhore, the rector of Whickham, were able to secure a lease from Bishop Hatfield lasting twelve years for an annual rent of £333 6s 8d. The operation was to be restricted to mining 20 tons per day, employing five barrowmen an output-per-man-shift which would be the envy of a modern colliery manager.

The economic potential of coal was

child putter 18th century

Riverside colliery 18th century

dependent upon a cheap mode of transport and in this respect nature had blessed Durham with two navigable rivers in the northern half of the county alongside which the coal seams were accessible.

By the fifteenth century both banks of Tyne and Wear were being exploited along their navigable lengths, the coal transported down the rivers in keels which could carry approximately 18 tons of coal. Once into deeper water the bounty was transferred to larger seagoing brigs and on to London. It was this method of transportation that gave 'sea-coal' its name.

Coal was first worked from the outcrop into the bankside of the river valleys to the limits of the ventilation. As these shallow drift mines became exhausted, shafts were sunk through the surface soils of clay and shale into the coal, to a depth no more than 30 feet or so. The coal was worked along the seam in all directions until heat and foul air made the pit unworkable, when it was abandoned. A new shaft was sunk further along the seam and the process repeated again and again until the seam became too deep for the technology of the time, when the area would be abandoned.

By the seventeenth century most of these easily accessible reserves had been fully exploited and deeper shafts had to be sunk further from the rivers. As the shafts became deeper, hand-operated gins were replaced with gins driven by horses. Ventilation remained the limiting factor

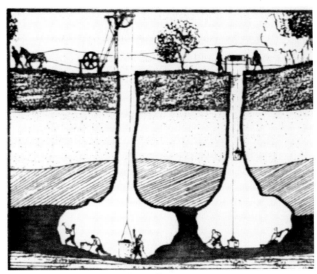

Bell pits

to the size of any operation. Fire damp (methane gas) and black damp (carbon-monoxide) were ever-present. The former would explode with devastating force while the latter would overcome and suffocate the unfortunate pitmen.

Towards the end of the century, pit working became more extensive and ventilation improved. A system of partitioning the workings was introduced into Durham's mines, which provided a continuous pathway for a current of air through the galleries. The air moved because a convection current was produced by a fire bucket suspended in one of two shafts. As air rose in the one shaft it descended the second, ventilating all parts of the mine. This simple method lasted in some pits until the twentieth century.

As pits became still deeper and more expensive to sink, a single shaft would be partitioned with wooden bratices into an upcast and downcast shaft.

Until the fifteenth century, the coal trade in Durham was dominated by the coal merchants of the river Tyne. Although coal was exported from the Wear, its shallow and narrow waters made it no serious rival.

In 1641 Scotland invaded Northumberland and Durham and its army occupied Newcastle until the Autumn of 1641. The punitive demands Scotland made on the region to maintain the occupation seriously damaged the coal trade, particularly on the Tyne.

In 1644 the Scottish army returned in support of Cromwell's revolution and the Parliament's forces put an embargo on all shipments of coal from Royalist Newcastle. Sunderland, which declared for Cromwell, benefited from the difficulties of its rival and the coal trade from Sunderland increased to fill the gap. For two years coal shipped from the Tyne declined to 10,000 chaldrons per year compared to the 80,000 chaldrons it had sustained for the former ten years.

Although Sunderland would never rival the dominance of the Tyne as a coal exporter, the years of 1644 to 1646 kick-started the Sunderland coal trade and by 1680 its coal exports rose from one twentieth to one third that of the Tyne.

Cromwell's revolution was the culmination of centuries of tension which developed between the complex layers within English feudal society as England's economy was transformed from one based on landed wealth and agriculture to dependence on trade and manufacture. Although Cromwell was motivated more by the interests of the merchants and emerging industrialists, the labouring classes had been inspired by his opposition to the authority of the Crown and saw Cromwell as liberator of all classes. They were disappointed. The Levellers and Diggers, sects based on the liberation of the lower classes, were persecuted once Cromwell's commonwealth was established.

Although serfdom had been abolished in the fifteenth century the agricultural labourer was far from free and was still tied to his master by legal contract and indenture.

In a sense, the mining of coal in Durham had developed out of agriculture. Coal was just another product yielded by the land and those who took it from the land were the former tillers. In many cases pitmen were both agricultural labourers and miners depending on the season. The 'bonny pit laddie' with his flowing locks, tight breeches and flowered waistcoat was a rural figure. His high days and holidays were firmly based in the old agricultural festivals and country fairs.

It is not surprising therefore that the contract between pitmen and master closely resembled the indentures of the agricultural labourer. This contract, known as the bond, tied the pitman to

Miner 18th century

his employer for a year. The penalties for breaking the bond were harsh fines and imprisonment.

Although the bond lasted for only a year, the masters were not slow to exploit ways and means of preventing their labourers moving on when it expired. Tied cottages, debt, and bonding day bounty were all inducements to make a temporary contract permanent in reality. In any case, the pitman who wished to terminate his employment had to get a 'Certificate of Leave' from his master. And no master would give such a certificate in times of labour shortage.

Bonding day, the one day pitmen were legally free, became crucial to the social and political development of Durham's pitmen. As the bonds became standardised and pitmen became more numerous, signing the bond became less of an individual act and more of a collective decision requiring organisation and discipline.

Bereft of any real legal rights or means of redress, pitmen's discontent would smoulder until hardship could be endured no longer. Collective action in the eighteenth century usually took the form of direct action. One of the many examples of this is described by Robert Colls in his book *The Pitmen of the Northern Counties*, based on the evidence given by two engine men employed by the owner of Newbottle colliery:

On 25 October 1731 Richard William Crofton, Thomas and John Bailey, Richard Oyston, William Davidson and one hundred other pitmen assembled at Newbottle colliery:

> Armed with staves forceable enter'd into the said Engine House broke several lead Pipes which the Engine was hindered from working & kept forceable Possession of ye said Engine House for a Night and a day and then gave Public Notice to these Informants that if the Engine was repaired or set to work before they had brought their masters to their Terms they wou'd pull it down to the Ground and Murder the said Informants . . . that these Informants made several Attempts to repair ye said Engine but were constantly disterb'd by ye said pitmen, so that the Engine continued unwrought for the space of three weeks. And the Steward of the Rt. Hon. the Earle of Scarborough was Obliged to Submit to the unreasonable Demands of the said Pitmen, Otherwise the Colliery wou'd have inevitably been drowned and lost.

Corf on tram

Wallsend spout - Drawn by R E Bewick

Pitmen were not the first to see the need for collective action. The coal owners had collaborated to control the labour market and restrict the sale of coal from the early part of the seventeenth century.

They were so successful in raising the price of coal on the streets of London that in 1638 a Bill was passed in the Star Chamber forcing the coal owners on the Tyne to 'Permit free trade' or 'bee taken into custody'. Despite the threats, the owners organised themselves to regulate the coal trade throughout the eighteenth and nineteenth centuries and to apportion to each a share of the trade in an operation known as the 'vend'.

In 1765 the owners agreed among themselves to force the pitmen to work past the bonding day, which was in September, a further twelve weeks into November. To force this measure on the pitmen the owners collectively agreed not to issue any certificates of leave, making it impossible for them to obtain employment. The pitmen refused to work under these conditions bringing the coal trade to an abrupt halt. Over 600 ships were trapped without cargoes in the Tyne and all the keelmen were idle. In total as many as 100,000 men were without work, either on strike or laid off.

When the masters relented and gave an assurance that leaving certificates would be issued and that men were free to seek employment at a colliery of their choice the pitmen responded by demanding that their bonds be cancelled and their wages increased. The owners refused.

Where the masters tried to restart the mines with blacklegs the pitmen responded violently, destroying pit headgear. On Pelton common the heapstead was set alight and barrels of burning pitch were thrown down the shaft. A company of dragoons was despatched into the area from York and by the end of September all collieries were back at work. No advance in wages was conceded but the pitmen had demonstrated that they were capable of resistance.

In the last decade of the eighteenth century mining was on the brink of a huge transformation. As early as 1729, steam power had been used in mines when Thomas Newcomen invented a crude steam engine to pump water out of Cornish tin mines. However, his engine was inefficient and could only produce straight-line motion. James Watt increased its efficiency in 1781 and, with the use of a crankshaft, transformed linear into circular motion.

By the start of the eighteenth century new and more efficient steam engines were developed, which greatly increased the ability to pump water and wind coal. In 1800 Philneas Crowther of Newcastle patented his vertical steam winding-engine. The tall winding houses of this new innovation would come to dominate the landscape of counties Durham and Northumberland. The last of his machines was still in use at Beamish Second pit in 1961.

At Cramlington colliery, Northumberland, George Stephenson was experimenting with his steam driven locomotives. In 1814 Blucher, his first engine, made its trial run.

The speed of development was breathtaking. The war with France had caused an escalation in the price of horses and the iron substitute was immediately welcomed by the coal owners. By 1815 the first crude locomotives of Stephenson and Hackworth were linking the pits of the Great Northern Coalfield. Within two decades railways were pushing out into the Russian Steppes and the North American Prairies. The battle for coal had developed steam power. Steam power changed industry forever and intensified the demand for coal.

When mines were sunk further and further from the rivers in the early part of the seventeenth century, intricate networks of wagon-ways linked the new sinkings to the rivers.

The surface of these wagon-ways fast became eroded by the passage of heavily laden chaldron wagons. Wooden and then iron rails were laid to increase the efficiency but each chaldron require a horse and this was both slow and expensive.

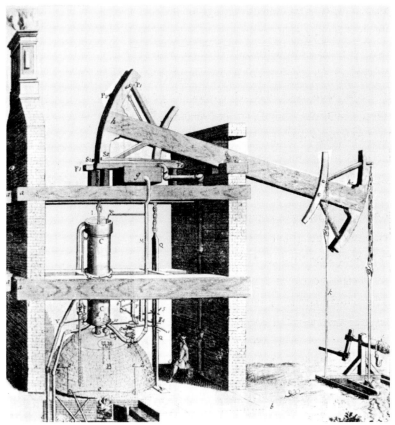

Atmospheric pump of the Newcomen type

At the turn of the nineteenth century the Tyne and Wear remained the main arteries of the coal trade but the increased demand for coal choked the rivers to the extent that cargoes were sometimes delayed for weeks. The new steam engines allowed the coal owners to circumnavigate the rivers and take the coal directly to the staithes at the river mouths. The days were numbered for the many thousands of keelmen who worked the rivers. They did not accept the new age of steam power gracefully and committed many acts of violence against the new machinery. On 20 March 1815 the keelmen of the Wear burned down the newly erected staithes at Sunderland and rioted. They were not dispersed until a party of dragoons arrived from Newcastle. Steam power did little to change the living conditions of the county's pitmen. Pit villages of that time were rough, the dwellings were jerry-built, thrown up by the coal owners at minimum expense. A miner's cottage consisted of one downstairs room; a ladder to the roof space provided a sleeping area. The walls were damp and roofs frail.

Sanitation was non-existent. Midden toilets were shared by several families. The human waste was dumped a short distance away in huge stinking ash heaps. The only drainage in the earthen lanes was an open ditch. When it rained the whole village was a sea of mud. In the heat of summer the smell of the middens and the dust were unbearable. Often just one communal well provided a whole village with water and may have been as far as a mile away.

Schools in pit villages were unheard of, deemed

Keelmen's strike 1822

The Street Pit Team Colliery - Sketch by T H Hair - etched by J Brown

by 'the better people' to be unnecessary when working life for pitmen's children could start at six or seven with a working day as long as seventeen hours. What time was there for school? And what learning was necessary for pit work?

What horrors a six-year-old child experienced the first day he was lowered down that dark shaft we can only imagine.

Pit villages were industrial ghettos in a rural setting. The physical isolation of the pit village made pitfolk a race apart from other classes of labouring poor. To the wealthy and the middle class these pitfolk were morally degenerate, over-indulgent where alcohol was concerned, fighters, gamblers, quarrelsome, foul-mouthed and rebellious. They were people of no value apart from their invaluable labour and their ability to breed the next generation of pitmen.

It was these very qualities, however, that attracted John Wesley in his campaign to save souls in the 1740s. He founded the Old Penshaw Methodist Society in 1742 and preached at Pelton in 1743. By the turn of the century Wesleyan societies were

Playing quoits

their spiritual, not economic, salvation. The Methodists' emphasis on a strong moral code, opposition to drink and belief in self fulfilment through hard work endeared them to some owners. But there is no doubt that the influence of Methodism on the northern pitmen created a feeling of self worth and confidence that was a catalyst for the development of trade unionism.

There was a strong influence of Methodism in the Brotherhood, a shadowy, semi-secret organisation of hewers that emerged amongst the pitmen of Northumberland and Durham in the latter years of the eighteenth century.

well established in the pit villages of the North East of England. They were never more than a minority sect, but the development of lay-preachers, and their system of Bible classes and prayer meetings injected small centres of literacy and organisation into what had been an overwhelmingly illiterate and unorganised community. Lay preachers toured a circuit of local societies creating a line of communication between the villages.

Wesley himself was a high Tory, a supporter of the establishment. His interest in the poor was

In 1793 Britain declared war with France. In the words of a contemporary poem it was a war to prove that 'One nation is brave and free'. But pitmen were denied this freedom. From the beginning of the war the Royal Navy Press gangs searched the ports and villages of the North East looking for free labour. By 1800 they had denuded the area of 3,000 hands, who had been persuaded, with the aid of a press gang's bludgeon, to seek a life at sea in the service of their king. Between the press gang and the recruiting sergeants they created a massive labour shortage which was to work in the pitmen's favour on binding day.

Binding day was a human market where men sold themselves for a year and, like every market, the law of supply and demand applied. Much as the coal owners tried to control the market, events slowly slipped out of their grasp. In 1799 an auction began of hewing prices and binding money as each owner tried to attract pitmen from another's colliery. At first the pitmen were slow to realise their advantage but as each binding day came round the pitmen held out longer for better terms. The binding season was by then in October, putting the pitmen in a strong bargaining position before the winter demand. By holding together they were welding themselves into a collective body. As at all times the most literate and articulate became leaders.

On 18 October 1804, as much as 21 guineas was being offered for every man who agreed to be bound. By 25 October the price in Northumberland was nearer thirty. For pitmen, used to only one or two

shillings bounty these must have been exhilarating times, an indication of how things could be. Those who had argued for combination during the dark years must have felt totally vindicated .

For the mine owners the 1804 binding was a financial disaster and they resolved to get their act together for the next year. They collectively agreed not to enter into competition for labour. Binding money would be standardised at 3 guineas. All collieries would bind simultaneously. No increases in hewing prices were to be offered, nor any other inducements of drink, food or clothing.

Colliers loading at Shields - Sketch by T H Hair

Labour itself was to be rationed. Just as food would be rationed in a famine so the mine owners would have their pitmen rationed. Each colliery was allocated a fixed number of men based upon the numbers hired over the previous three years. If new collieries were opened then each existing colliery had to take a proportional reduction to supply labour for the new winnings.

As the October binding approached the Brotherhood drew up a list of demands to be incorporated in their new bonds and on binding day they marched with their demands to Newcastle. For two weeks the men held out on the streets of Newcastle demanding the terms of their petition, to no avail. The solidarity of the employers was not breached and finally the men bound on the employers' terms.

The year 1806 saw further reductions in binding money and by 1807 the owners were operating their own strike fund to help companies beat the organisation of the Brotherhood. In some cases the rules on paying higher binding money were relaxed to help owners break the pitmen's solidarity.

The pitmen of the Northern Coalfield had suffered five consecutive years of reductions and strict control. While unions for the miners were illegal under the Combination Acts of 1799 and 1800

the coal owners had no such problems. The Coal Owners' Committee was highly organised. They jealously controlled the amount of coal mined through the 'vend', and conspired together to regulate the rates of pay for their pitmen. The powers of the Brotherhood were at a low ebb.

Flushed with success, the owners decided to force home their advantage even further by changing the date of the binding day from October to January. The October binding day coincided with the start of the winter demand for coal, which was to the men's advantage. If they held out for better terms the employers would lose money immediately. In the event of the miners refusing to be bound, the owners' first line of attack was to turn the pitmen from their homes. While living in camps by the roadside was uncomfortable in Autumn it was near fatal in midwinter.

In 1809 the owners collectively agreed to move the binding date from October to January. This was at first accepted without opposition in 1809 but in 1810 when the owners again insisted on a January binding the pitmen rose up in revolt, invigorating the Brotherhood. Until this time they were a loose, shadowy and, in fact, illegal organisation. The risk of imprisonment under the Combination Acts was very real. One way of avoiding the Act was to register as a friendly society and on 24 October 1810 the Brethren of the Colliers Fund was registered in Gateshead. Other local branches were to follow.

Changing the binding day was not the only cause of opposition to the bond of that year. The bond itself was new and included many complicated clauses, drawn up by the owners' barrister, including draconian fines for misdemeanours.

Despite their opposition the men bound themselves until January 1811, but by October 1810 the pitmen were in open revolt and the Brotherhood led a wave of strikes.

Over 30 collieries immediately responded to the call of the Brothers. The authorities responded by arresting the men they thought were the leaders. Both the jail and the House of Correction in Durham City were soon full and the Bishop of Durham kindly lent the authorities his stables where the human overflow from the jail was chained to the stalls and guarded by the Durham Volunteers and the special constables.

That the established church should lend itself to such oppression may seem incredible. However the Bishop of Durham's support for the owners in the first decade of the nineteenth century was quite natural. The Bishop of Durham, still then a Prince of the Realm, was the fattest of coal owners and probably received more revenue from the coal trade than any other single owner. As the biggest land owner in the county huge sums of money filled the coffers of the Dean and Chapter, either from direct ownership of the mines or through royalties and way-leaves. By imprisoning pitmen the Bishop was merely protecting the church's investments.

He was not likely to lose any parishioners by his actions since at that time the appearance of a miner in a Church of England was a very rare occurrence. In Durham the established

Illustration - Ann Wood

churches were always situated within the old agricultural villages. When the mine owners built new industrial villages around the pit-heads of the new sinking they were often remote from older settlements. Clergy more used to the genteel rigours of rural life rarely ventured into the hubbub of the pit villages. The spiritual vacuum thus created had been filled by John Wesley's preachers. If they had a religion at all, miners practised it in the hungry little chapels of the Wesleyan Methodists.

Despite the partiality of the Bishop, however, it was a Church of England vicar, the Rev. William

Nesfield of Chester le Street, who was sufficiently moved by the plight of the miners to intervene. He agreed to intercede on behalf of the men if they would agree to honour the terms of the bond until January 1811. By mid-January a compromise was reached, with the owners agreeing to a 5 April binding day.

The Committee of Coal Owners, ever conscious of the compromise forced upon them and the tactical advantage conceded, recorded in their minute book that this date was not just convenient for the removal of the miners' families from their houses but also coincided with the commencement of the cultivation of their gardens.

In 1807 an event occurred on a windswept fellside in Lancashire which was to have a profound influence among the pitmen of Durham. Two dissenting Methodist preachers had summoned their flock to a camp on the slopes of Mow Cop. They had quarrelled with the elders of the Wesleyan Methodists and were in no mood for compromise. The Methodist movement, unlike the established Church of England from which it sprung, was ferociously evangelical. While they believed in saving the soul of the labouring poor through their missionary work, they inherited from the mother church the desire for hierarchical control and strict adherence to a set prayer book. When he died in 1791 Wesley left his

Durham Jail under Elvet Bridge

unmistakable stamp of deference to authority and loyalty to the established order. The Leeds conference in 1791 declared 'unfeigned loyalty to the King and sincere attachment to the Constitution'.

The dissenting preachers Hugh Bourne and William Clowes had other ideas. For them no prayer book was necessary. If God was everywhere, they argued, then he was in the room with you, and you could address him directly, choosing whatever words came to mind. Their God was not a God of the establishment but a God of the poor. They trawled the Bible for quotations supporting their belief that God was on the side of the oppressed and against the tyranny of the rich. Their style of preaching was robust: not for them the carefully chosen words of the country vicar. They were noisy, they shouted, and they sang lustily, adopting the popular tunes of the day for their hymns. They were the newborn fundamentalists of their day and well deserved the nickname 'Ranters'. They converted by engendering a collective hysteria. When a sinner was moved to see the light he would shake and swoon and often fall over backwards, with injury.

In 1811 they became a fully fledged offshoot, a 'connexion' as they called it, of Methodism. The were by no means the first to break away. In the

Miners in Bishop's stables - Illustration by Anne Wood

history of Methodism there were many sects: the Independents, Unitarians, New Connexion Methodists, Tent Methodists, Quaker Methodists, even Magic Methodists, and a group known as the Welsh Jumpers. But none were to have such an effect on the Durham miners as the Primitive Methodists.

Nine years later in 1820 Clowes and his missionaries entered the county of Durham and established a bridgehead in the tiny village of Ingelton in the lower reaches of Teesdale. In summer the next year they moved up the Tees valley among the lead miners, establishing small groups of followers in each village. They crossed over the moors to Weardale where they were even more successful. By the following year they had traversed the Durham coalfield to the towns of South Shields and Sunderland. In 1822, probably in the village of Hetton, that they met and converted a 26-year-old Thomas Hepburn.

Thomas was born in Pelton in 1796, the son of a pitman. At the age of eight his father was killed in a pit accident and, to support the family, Tom started work at Urpeth Colliery in 1804. He moved from Pelton to Lamb's colliery, Fatfield, and when the owner was declared bankrupt, moved to Jarrow for a year before being attracted to a new sinking by the Hetton Coal Company between the villages of Hetton and Easington Lane.

The Hetton Coal company had been formed in 1820 by Arthur Mowbray and the wealthy landowner, Sir Archibald Cochrane. Together they were able to attract London finance to a venture that was fraught with dangers. In sinking Hetton colliery they were making the third attempt to reach coal beneath the limestone of East Durham's concealed coalfield. The danger came from the Sand Feeder, an unstable area of sand and water beneath the limestone. Their efforts were not welcomed by other owners in the area who saw the new company as a threat to their carefully controlled monopoly. Despite opposition from Lords Londonderry and Lambton, and the water of the Sand Feeder, the colliery opened in 1822 and drew its first coals in 1823.

Thomas Hepburn may well have hewed the first coal to reach the surface, but by now he had other things on his mind. He had married in 1820, he was now a Primitive Methodist lay preacher, and he was attending night classes to further his education.

Although an educated pitmen was at this time something of a rare animal, Hepburn was by no means alone in his thirst for education. Richard Fynes in his *History of the Northumberland and Durham Miners* refers to a miner living in the Hetton area at this time by the name of Mackintosh:

> . . . a bold honest intelligent man . . . [who] felt the degraded state of his fellow men and set about the great social work of co-operation with the view to the amelioration of himself and his companions.

Their is no record of any connection between Hepburn and Mackintosh but living in a small community and sharing the same values it is inconceivable that they did not collaborate and have a mutual influence on each other.

Efforts by Mackintosh to begin a co-operative movement, however, came unstuck in the teeth of determined opposition of the owners and the suspicions of the community in general. He was accused of dishonesty and left to start a new life in America.

Hetton colliery - Drawing by F D Harding

As a hewer Thomas had a relatively short working day, probably no more than eight hours. It was normal for a colliery to work with two shifts of hewers. Since they were paid by the volume of coal they hewed the length of the hewers' shift was of less consequence to the owners. Each had only a certain amount of energy per day and the shorter the period of time he released that energy the greater the advantage to the owner. On the other hand the back-bye pitmen who serviced the hewers had to cover two shifts by working sixteen hours per day. The hewers made up the majority of the men; they earned the most and consequently were the first to feel the effects of a reduction in prices.

The short shift of the hewers gave them a degree of leisure time unequalled by other classes of manual workers. The majority of pitmen spent their time in rural pursuit, tending their gardens, walking, poaching, dog- and cockfighting and, of course, drinking to excess.

Drunkenness had always been a problem in the pit villages. When life could be taken away in the flash of a methane explosion or the sudden collapse of a faulted roof, miners lived for the

Richard Fynes

moment. As a lay preacher, Tommy Hepburn railed against the evils of drink, appealed to men to put their trust in God and their own salvation, through education and unionism.

The Primitives adopted the same type of organisation as the Wesleyans. A limited number of professional preachers would train and instruct an army of amateur, or lay, preachers, each part of a plan within a circuit of chapels covering up to twenty-five miles, depending on the population density. Each lay preacher would preach in a different village each Sunday.

As Hepburn walked between the villages attending to his preaching he established contact with like-minded men. The chapels became central to the organisation of the union. Whereas there is no doubt that the old Brotherhood had been influenced by Methodism, the Primitive Methodist chapels became the central driving force of the union: Primitive Methodism became a union religion.

In 1825 after the repeal of the Combinations Acts the Brotherhood emerged from illegality into the broad light of day. The union was given a new name 'The Colliers of the United Association of Durham and Northumberland' and they published their grievances in a pamphlet entitled *A Voice from the Coal Mines*. The village of Hetton in County Durham was to become the recognised centre of this new pitmen's union and Thomas Hepburn its undisputed leader. Although Thomas was a Primitive Methodist preacher he was no isolated prophet beamed down from above. His outlook on life was determined by ideas that had been fermenting within the lower ranks of society for the previous four decades. The working class as we understand it was in its infancy and the idea that this class had rights was an entirely new concept.

When, in 1791, Thomas Paine published his book, *The Rights of Man*, he raised a banner around which working people could rally. Here, at last were carefully worked arguments against the despotism of kings and corrupt ministers, arguments which called for definite democratic rights for the ordinary working people. Paine, an Englishman and former Exciseman, wrote from the safe haven of the newly independent states of North America. His book sold in its thousands and was, predictably, banned by George III's nervous government.

Underground explosion

If the defeat of the King's army by the North American rebels had shaken the British aristocracy in 1780, then the French Revolution eleven years later struck terror into its heart and made it view the growing dissent amongst the lower classes with renewed alarm.

Those who opposed the King's government during these years were generally known as Radicals and were organised in a diverse number of illegal, locally based societies and clubs. Opinions within radical circles were as diverse as the social background of their members. There were those who advocated the removal of the King's government by physical force and others who sought reform through the political process (however corrupt and inadequate that process might be). There were those who held the views of the French Rationalists and denied the existence of God, and others who were fanatical Christians. Some were Republican and others advocated a reformed monarchy.

Individuals within the ranks of the newly rich industrialists and even, in some cases, the aristocracy were won over to the ideas of reform more by an instinct for survival than any principals of egalitarianism. The aristocratic Lord Lambton himself was known as 'Radical Jack' and on one occasion in 1819 led a band of keelmen to smash a Loyalist address in Sunderland.

Newcastle was a centre of radical dissent. Thomas Spence, a Newcastle born schoolmaster, was the founder of one of the most extreme factions of the Radical Movement. He went one step further than Paine by calling for the land to be taken from the aristocracy and the formation of land co-operatives. As early as 1775, Spence had given his first lecture to the Newcastle Philosophical Society on the subject of agrarian socialism. These views proved too strong for the more conservative membership, who expelled him from the society. He later left Newcastle to continue his agitation in London.

During the years of the Napoleonic Wars, the Newcastle engraver and Radical, Thomas Bewick,

Thomas Hepburn

recalled regular meetings with a 'set of staunch advocates of the liberties of mankind' in the Blue Bell, the Unicorn and the News Room. He described his associates as tradesmen of a genteel sort who were, 'men of sense and consequence: bankers' clerks, artisans and agents, and included a shoemaker, a builder, a founder, a white-smith, an editor, a fencing master, a radical gentleman and several actors'. The overwhelming majority of the labouring poor, however, were excluded from this debate by their illiteracy, yet they played a crucial part when their smouldering discontent erupted into tumult and riot.

In 1815, the battle of Waterloo brought to an end twenty-three years of almost continuous war. The war had kept food prices high and labour in great demand. With its end economic disaster fell upon the working classes and the growing ranks of the unemployed were swelled by soldiers returning from active duty.

As the price of corn fell, the Government passed the Corn Laws forbidding the importation of cheap foreign grain into Britain. Only when the price of home grown corn rose to a level acceptable to the land owners could grain be imported. As this Bill was being passed, the House of Commons had to be defended by armed soldiers; such was the opposition of the ordinary people. In England bread was still the staple diet

Tom Paine

of the poor; unlike the Irish, they had not yet been forced to eat potatoes.

In 1816 a further burden was added to the distress of the poor when, in an attempt to placate the middle classes, the Government abolished income tax which had been introduced during the war years. By their poverty the poor had been excluded from paying this tax, but they could not avoid the indirect taxes introduced as a consequence of its abolition, particularly for such essentials as hops, vital in brewing 'The Drink'.

A wave of unrest was inevitable. A demobilised army, cheated of its pensions and without work, poverty, mass unemployment, and towns seething with radical dissent, proved an explosive mixture that tipped the balance in favour of physical force and away from peaceful persuasion. The labouring classes swelled the ranks of the Radicals, pikes were made in the workshops of the rebellious artisans. Armed bands roamed the countryside seizing the firearms of yeomen farmers. It was even possible for a poor man to purchase a pike by paying in instalments, an early form of the 'never, never'.

The government, well practised in the art of espionage, infiltrated the movement with paid spies experienced in the art of provocation. On the night of 9 June 1817, three hundred men armed with pikes gathered in the Derbyshire village of Pentridge under the leadership of Jeremiah Brandreth. They were convinced that a general uprising had been organised. They marched the fifteen miles to Nottingham, anticipating that when they arrived the city would already be in the hands of the revolutionaries. Instead they were met by a force of Hussars. They were rounded up and the leaders were subsequently hanged: they had been urged into action and then betrayed by a government spy.

The hanging of the Pentridge leaders, the

widespread revulsion at the government's use of spies and the continued distress in the country only poured fuel on to the fire. The manufacture of pikes and the late night drilling continued. George III and his government had a big problem in controlling what they called 'the mob'. These were the days before a regular police force was common in most parts of Britain. Keeping the peace was the duty of magistrates appointed from the ranks of the gentry and the wealthy. In Durham and Northumberland they were almost always coal owners, their agents, or close business associates. Magistrates had the power to recruit special constables to enforce order, but these part timers were untrained, ill-armed and, in general, ineffective. The final and often the only solution was to call for the assistance of the military.

Throughout the eighteenth century the emerging working class, bereft of any democratic voice or organisation, tended to show its dissatisfaction by resorting to violence. The spontaneous strikes of pitmen and keelmen almost always resulted in riots and extensive damage to the masters' property. As the process of the law always lagged behind events the authorities were powerless to prevent this damage. Even when the army was called upon it could be days before they arrived on the scene of the riot. The perpetrators were often long gone and retribution could only then be effected on the dubious testimony of informers induced by the promise of a reward.

Towards the end of the eighteenth century working-class violence became more controlled and the practice of holding a mass demonstration emerged as a show of strength and a threat: concede to our just demands or you know what we will do, we will destroy your property. In this situation there were crude rules of engagement. The military could not charge a demonstration until the Riot Act had been read by a magistrate or army officer. Often the very reading of the Act could provoke a riot.

On 16 August 1819 on St. Peter's Fields, Manchester, after four years of unrest, the government decided to get in first and teach the Radicals and Reformers a lesson they would not be likely to forget.

A huge mass meeting had been called. For weeks a hostile press had been goading the Radicals and Reformers, describing them as a rabble, ill-clad and unwashed. It was the wish of the Constitutionalists, a more moderate wing of the Radical movement, to contradict this unkind characterisation of their followers. The organisers called for 'cleanliness, sobriety and order' in the appearance and conduct of the participants.

Their orderly conduct and peaceful intent was

demonstrated by the presence of women and children among the thousands who came to listen to Henry Hunt, one of the most prominent of the Radical leaders. This did not impress the ranks of the Manchester Yeomanry who charged, killing eleven and injuring hundreds. Within days the whole country knew of the outrage and an avalanche of revulsion swept through the country.

On 11 October 1819 an estimated 50 to 100,000 pitmen, keelmen, seamen, iron workers, and others marched through Newcastle to a protest meeting on the Town Moor where they were addressed by leading Radicals. The wonted violence of the Manchester Yeomanry gave the Radicals the moral high ground and they were keen not to relinquish it. This massive meeting was uncharacteristically disciplined. Pitmen, keelmen and sailors heeded the calls for restraint, all shunned the drink and marched in disciplined formation to the Town Moor.

They returned to their villages in the same disciplined manner. Three days later, however, it was a different story. The keelmen of the Tyne clashed with the marines on the Quayside. The order to fire was given and a keelmen was shot dead.

The burgers of Newcastle and the mayor in

Peterloo massacre

particular were by now firmly convinced that they were faced with revolution and they organised their own armed association. They desperately clamoured for the assistance of the military, warning Home Secretary Sidmouth that the keelmen, seamen and pitmen were drilling and arming. Even when the keelmen returned to work in November it did nothing to quiet the fears of the magistrates. Magistrate Thorp of Ryton reported that the pitmen were planning to take middle-class hostages, particularly ladies, with them on their demonstrations as a protection against suffering a military charge. Between 11 November and 19 December the Mayor of Newcastle sent five letters to Sidmouth describing the pitmen as proto-revolutionaries who were in possession of gunpowder and fully armed.

These events injected radicalism into the lives of the miners of Northumberland and Durham. Radical classes were organised in Jarrow, Sheriff Hill, South Shields, Winlaton and Sunderland and, according to a contemporary reporter, the radical newspaper, *The Black Dwarf,* 'could be seen in the hat-crown of almost every pitman you met'.

While the northern pitmen were organising their radical classes a group of desperate 'Old Radicals' were meeting in a garret in Cato Street, London, under the leadership of Arthur Thistlewood, a gentleman very much down on his luck. He had served as an officer in the French wars with distinction and was noted as one of the best swordsmen in Europe. Smarting at accusations by Henry Hunt of being a government spy, Thistlewood calculated that if he and his fellow conspirators could pull off one spectacular blow against the establishment, the whole country would rise up in rebellion. Throughout January and February 1820 they devised a plan to murder the cabinet while they dined, then to place the heads of Castlereagh and Sidmouth on pikes and declare a Provisional Government.

Unfortunately the conspirators had taken into their confidence a man called Edwards who really was a spy. Thistlewood and his men were arrested, but not before Thistlewood 'ran through' a Bow Street

Henry Hunt

Runner. This debacle was all the government required to pass repressive measures through parliament and to turn the tide against the dissenters. Thistlewood and his companions perished on the scaffold with defiant dignity. They all refused the consolation of a priest, except one called Davidson , who was a black Jamaican and a Methodist.

By the end of 1820 the pikes were put away and the drilling stopped. It is safe to assume that five years later when the new pitmen's union was formed these events were weighing heavily in the mind of Thomas Hepburn. The loose coalition of Radical and Reformist leaders had proved hopelessly disunited. Organised physical resistance was vulnerable to the spy system, and the government had proved totally ruthless in its recourse to the 'steel lozenger' and the gallows. Hepburn's future appeals to pitmen to shun violence may well have been influenced more by fear of government reprisal than an ideological conviction.

The new found legality of the pitmen's union allowed it to publish its propaganda and increase its membership. The continued slump in the sale of coal, however, ensured that the union was unable make any radical changes to the quality of life. The main tactic of the union, no doubt influenced by the owners' practice of controlling

IT being thought expedient, at this Period, by many of the Inhabitants of this Town, to form an ARMED ASSOCIATION, for the Protection of Property, in Aid of the Civil Power; such Persons as wish to enrol themselves, for that Purpose, are informed, that they may enter their Names and Places of Residence in a Book, which will lie at the Exchange, Sandhill, until the 28th Instant in the Evening, when the List will be closed.

Newcastle,
25th October, 1819.

output through the vend, was to restrict output. Hewers would be restricted to hewing a set volume of coal, guaranteeing them a fixed income. Where a dispute arose at a particular pit, the whole membership of the union would be levied to maintain the members out on strike. The union was at first a hewers' union but this was to change and the base of the membership broadened to encompass all classes of miners and boys.

In 1826 the owners fired a warning shot across the bows of the union by introducing a standard bond. The union was as yet not universally accepted by all pitmen and the standard bond undermined the hit-and-run tactics of the union. The union pits made a stand but the action was short lived and by the end of April 1826 all pits had bound.

Far from improving, the coal trade deteriorated and by 1830 there was serious distress throughout the two counties. The owners contemplated reducing the pitmen's wages, a measure that occasioned the Duke of Wellington to caution his friend Lord Londonderry on the consequences of such a course of action. Wellington was not, however, interested in the welfare of the miners, but feared the consequences of their resistance. Anticipating the need for troops to keep order in the coalfield, he reminded his friend that troops cost money and money meant taxes.

If Thomas Hepburn came to epitomise the values of trade unionism, then Londonderry and his family became, for miners, the hate figure of the nineteenth century. Londonderry, formerly Lord Stewart, was from the Anglo-Irish Stewart family. He had seen service with the Duke of Wellington in the Peninsular Wars before becoming British Ambassador in Vienna. He was not a wealthy man but married the wealthy heiress, Lady Frances Ann Vane-Tempest, on 3 April 1819, when she was at the tender age of nineteen. Lady Frances was a ward in Chancery. Her relations opposed the marriage and managed to tie up a large portion of her wealth in a trust beyond the reach of her new husband.

On the death of his half-brother, Lord Castlereagh, Stewart became the third Marquis of Londonderry in 1822. He resigned his post in Vienna and returned to London where he and his wife dazzled society with their opulent display of wealth and extravagance. Lady Frances earned a considerable income from the collieries she owned in the mid-Durham area of Pittington and Rainton. A quarter million tons of coal from these collieries were transported overland to the staithes at Penshaw, where they were loaded into keels and floated down the Wear to Sunderland, to be transferred to seagoing colliers for export.

By the early part of the century, the Wear was becoming extremely congested and coal shipments were often delayed by weeks. It was also a very expensive method of transport which Londonderry estimated was costing £10,000 per year. His solution was to build a new port at Seaham linked by rail to his collieries in mid-Durham.

The Manor of Seaham was at that time owned by Sir Ralph Milbanke, whose daughter, Nancy, had married Lord Byron in 1815. He had mortgaged his land in order to pay a dowry of £20,000 to Byron. No doubt under financial pressure

Milbanke put his land up for auction in October 1821 and it subsequently fell into the hands of Londonderry. On the 28 November 1828, Londonderry laid the foundation stone of his new harbour.

While Londonderry had acquired his wife's mines and the revenue they created, her capital was beyond his reach. To finance this venture Londonderry borrowed heavily from his London bankers. A third player in this drama was Londonderry's viewer, John Buddle. Mineowners relied entirely upon their viewers for the day-to-day running of the mines. Viewers were in charge of every aspect of the mines' production and they determined the profitability of the concern. Buddle, like most in his profession, was a self-made man. In those days there were no university courses in mining engineering. The innovations in engineering were developed by trial and error and the inspiration of working men. Buddle himself had developed a method of ventilation and 'bord and pillar extraction' that became known as the Buddle method. While Buddle was Londonderry's viewer, he did not work exclusively for Londonderry, but was engaged by owners on the Tyne and had his own mining investments.

By 1831, the miners of Durham and Northumberland were at the end of their tether.

Third Marquis of Londonderry statue in front of Londonderry's Seaham offices

For fifteen years the coal trade had lurched from one crisis to another and each time the price of coal fell it was the pitmen who had suffered the brunt of the recession. The terms of the bond had gradually deteriorated and binding money, which had reached the dizzy heights of 30 guineas in the boom of 1800, was but a distant memory for most pitmen. Where it existed at all it was no more than a shilling. The meagre pay was stolen back by the owners through unfair fines or robbed in the company stores known as Tommy Shops.

On 12 March 1830, the union called a huge meeting at Black Fell near Eighton Banks on the raised ground above where the Angel of the North stands today. Nine days later on 21 March, twenty thousand pitmen met on the Town Moor, Newcastle, where they passed a number of resolutions calling for higher pay and a reduction in the hours of work for children. They called for a levy of all pitmen in order to petition parliament and decided that they would not be bound in the coming April. If the employers agreed, they would work unbound. If not, they would refuse to work.

The coalowners were still highly organised by the 'Committee' which jealously controlled production through the vend. Their first response was a cautious acceptance that the hours of the children should be reduced from seventeen hours a day to something more civilised, perhaps twelve. But they were adamant that the terms of the bond would remain. The men refused to be bound under the old terms and from 5 April they were effectively locked out.

Throughout Northumberland and Durham the union was organised with a branch at each pit which elected delegates to an area committee. For the purpose of running the strike Hepburn set up his headquarters in the Cock public house in Newcastle, where the delegates and executive committee met. In his letters to Londonderry Buddle described Hepburn's committee as the 'Cock Parliament'.

The leaders of the union cautioned the pitmen to conduct themselves in a non-violent manner but, faced with the intransigence of the owners, violence did erupt. In the Blyth and Bedlington, where blacklegs were working, the pit-head machinery was sabotaged and corves were thrown down the shaft. There were similar disturbances on the Wear.

Richard Fynes in his *History of the Northumberland and Durham Miners* describes how,

> Large bodies of violent and lawless men traversed the country doing a great many extravagant acts, and doing much silly and unjustifiable mischief.

Special constables were sworn in and the Northumberland and Newcastle Yeomanry were called out. The Yeomanry were the irregulars drawn from the ranks of property owners, gentleman farmers, and rich traders. It was the

Manchester Yeomanry that had charged at Peterloo and throughout the country the Yeomanry were both hated and held in contempt. The regular forces of the 82nd Regiment of foot were more feared and respected. They were stationed at Sunderland Barracks and were dispatched to Hetton, the recognised heartland of the union. A party of marines set sail from Portsmouth for the Tyne on news of the disturbances. For the first time, the coalowners' committee was faced with a united and defiant body of men.

At first Buddle had thought that a rift would soon develop between the union leadership and the men but he had to grudgingly admit that there was 'a powerful sprit that bound the men together'.

Unfortunately for the coalowners the collective spirit of survival on this occasion eluded them. Londonderry was in big trouble. He was heavily in debt to the London banks, the men he sarcastically called his Quaker friends. He feared that these bankers would take advantage of his situation and, by calling in the loans, gain title to his mines. He agreed to meet the miners' delegates and accepted their terms. The union delegates were astounded by their success and, although they had wanted a county-wide agreement, they changed tactics and allowed the men at the Londonderry collieries to bind under the new terms if they paid one quarter of their earnings to support the men still locked out. Buddle was incensed by Londonderry's breach of faith and

Child labour in mines

feared that his own reputation in the trade would suffer as a result of his connection with Londonderry. Buddle and the Tyne owners held firm but, to their consternation, Lord Lambton, also heavily in debt to the banks, immediately started to bind his men on the new terms.

Once Londonderry's men resumed production he began to produce himself out of debt with little regard for the vend or the plight of the owners who were holding firm. As the remaining owners stared ruin in the face, the dominoes started to fall and some owners even reintroduced binding money of up to 2 guineas. When finally Buddle's collieries on the Tyne collapsed, he was unexpectedly elevated from a villain, who was 'booed and hissed at everywhere he went', to a hero who had 'fought like a man'.

In a letter to Londonderry he describes how he was forcibly chaired by a cheering crowd of pitmen in Wallsend and how he had to abscond the following day to avoid being 'drawn in honour' in a victory procession from Wallsend to Newcastle. He was equally disturbed when his nephew, the under-viewer at Percy Main was forced to 'carouse' with his pitmen in a victory celebration.

The whole coalfield was now in a state of excitement and celebration. Unionism had achieved its first undisputed victory. In the months before the lockout, blacksmiths, joiners and other crafts had joined the union. Now deputies and overmen were following suit. The union was extending its influence even outside the collieries and there was talk of farm workers joining and the union fixing the prices of commodities in the shops.

At the pits they began to control how the pit was run, how much coal a hewer could hew. They curtailed the actions of the officials and in some cases called for the removal of unpopular officials. They would not allow the employment of anyone who was not 'a regular-bred pitman'. This was all too much for John Buddle who, by the end of June 1831, suffered a complete breakdown. The union was well established and in control. Inspired by their victory the union expanded its ranks to take in the more privileged overmen, deputies and waste workers.

The owners were running scared and were already plotting their revenge. On 13 August 1831, fired up by their victory, the pitmen's union held a big meeting on Boldon Fell in support of the Reform Bill which had begun its passage through parliament. Miners who had been a part of the radical dissent between 1815-19 saw the limited reforms within this Bill as a step towards the emancipation of the working classes. Pitmen

Pelton colliery - T E Hair

marched to this meeting in their thousands, behind bands and banners. We can imagine the atmosphere full of optimism and celebration. This was not a time for dissent, the union had been established; the masters had seen reason and given in to the union's just demands. The King had given his support to the Reform Bill which must, they thought, get rid of corruption.

The first business of the meeting was to elect Hepburn as a full time official of the union, charged with the task of enforcing the rules and encouraging the establishment of new branches The national anthem was then played and the King was congratulated in having the excellent ministers, Gray, Broughton and Durham. They were congratulating Durham, the very coal owner with whom they had been locked in conflict. But why not? They had fought fair and, as far as the pitmen were concerned, they harboured no hard feelings. Had they not invited the viewers to their victory celebrations?

It was soon to transpire that this feeling of conciliation was not shared by the owners. The first warning shots were fired in December 1831 when a dispute arose at Waldridge colliery over the introduction of lead miners into the pit. While thirty or so of these lead miners were working down the mine, a huge crowd of a thousand miners gathered at bank and stopped the pumping engine. Tubs and cisterns were thrown down the shaft, putting the lives of the lead miners in great danger.

A huge reward of 250 guineas was offered for the apprehension of the ringleaders and at the Spring Assizes of 1832 six miners were convicted and imprisoned for periods of six to eighteen months. Predictably, the authorities confused the leaders of the violence with the leaders of the union and it was widely accepted that the only crime of the men was that of being union men. Hepburn publicly opposed such acts of violence and cautioned against allowing frustrations to get out of control. For him, self-education and sobriety were the way towards freedom. He advocated the provision of village libraries maintained by pitmen's subscriptions and never tired of predicting the advantages that knowledge would bring to pitmen.

The existence of large numbers of poor lead miners in the Pennine hills was a constant threat to the pitmen of Durham and Northumberland. Lead mining had prospered in the west of Durham, North Yorkshire, and Cumberland throughout the seventeenth century. The working conditions of lead miners differed from those of coal miners.

The coal miner was tied to the pit by the bond and, if he was a hewer, was paid by the quantity of coal he produced in a fortnight and usually worked alongside many pitmen who shared the same conditions. Living in close-knit communities, a natural cohesion bound pitmen together.

In contrast, the Pennine lead miners were free agents who combined in small groups, often members of the same family. These groups were essentially subcontractors who would enter into a contract with the owners. The contract established a price by weight for the ore which was won over a period of a quarter. Payment would be made at the end of the quarter.

Lead mining was much more of a gamble. The veins of lead could suddenly disappear or degenerate into yields not worth mining. It was not unusual for a lead miner to work a full three months and end up in debt to the company for the cost of gun powder. To sustain himself and his family through the quarter he would be dependent upon small grants of land where his wife and children would rear a pig and a few sheep, rather like the Scottish crofters.

Small groups of lead miners worked in isolation up on the fells, sleeping in insanitary shelters called shops, and not returning to their families until the weekend.

The Letch pit near Hetton - T E Hair

The lead miner had a shorter life expectancy than the coal miner. Although his galleries were free from gas and the roofs were stronger and less prone to collapse, the poisonous effects of the lead and stone dust destroyed his body more quickly. In general the lead miner on his Pennine fell was poorer than his cousin on the coal field. His life was uncertain and to the coal miner he was a threat.

In the January 1832, more lead miners were imported to Coxlodge and Kenton collieries. The union, who had decreed that only 'pure-bred pitmen' should be employed, supported the men when they refused to work alongside the lead miners. The employers retaliated by turning the men out of their houses in mid-winter.

Faced with the threat of a united and confident workforce, the owners put behind them the wrangles of the previous year and united against Hepburn and his union, setting up a fighting fund to smash the union. Each owner was taxed 2 per cent of all sales to meet the cost of importing lead miners and holding out against the union.

The Coxlodge and Kenton men held out for two months until the union had to concede and allow the men to seek work at other collieries. Despite this setback, Hepburn's union remained confident that they could build on the success of the previous year and win further concessions. As the yearly bindings approached the union held a mass meeting on Boldon Fell on 3 March to discuss the terms upon which they would be prepared to bind.

The owners' committee, however, had their own plans with regard to the terms of the new bond and declared in mid-March, when the bonds were first read, that no keeker or deputy would be bound if they were members of the union.

At a mass meeting on April 14 at Blackfell the men pledged themselves to remain loyal to the union. Hepburn called for a sacrifice that would make a great difference in twelve months time. When only half the collieries reached agreement and bound, Hepburn employed the same tactics that had been so successful in 1831: settling where possible and taxing the working miners to finance those on strike.

By the end of April the owners counter-attacked

by refusing to bind union delegates. By 4 May the owners were more confident and declared that they would not bind any man who was a member of the union and drew up a declaration of fidelity which all workers had to sign, renouncing union membership before they could be employed.

Knowing that the bound miners were paying a quarter of their earnings to the unbound men the owners conspired to restrict the earnings of the miners to 3 shillings per day, an amount well below the restriction of 4 shillings and 6 pence imposed by the union.

The owners' committee knew well that Hetton was the stronghold of the union and if the union was to be smashed then Hetton and Hepburn's vanguard had to be smashed first. A contingent of metropolitan police were drafted into the village assisted by special constables and a contingent of the Queen's Bays. The men who were not members of the union were issued with arms for their own protection.

With the village heavily occupied by the military, the specials and the Metropolitan police, and the blacklegs armed, the owners orchestrated a reign of terror. Where more than one or two men gathered together they were arrested and tied up in the colliery stables and workshops. Cutlasses and pistols were thrust in their faces to provoke and intimidate them. Men who were active in the union were singled out for special treatment and these marked men were the first to be evicted from their houses to make way for the blacklegs.

Mathias Dunn, the viewer at Hetton colliery, had concluded in the first week of April that he would have to import labour if the union was to be broken, and set off by coach to Teesdale. He travelled to Barnard Castle and on to Middleton-in-Teesdale, where he addressed a meeting of two hundred lead miners.

It was to accommodate these miners that the evictions began in Hetton on 21 April, starting with the families of the marked men. The evictions proceeded without any retaliation but that night a blackleg called Errington was found shot dead. He had been an ardent advocate of the union but had succumbed to pressure from the owners and bound.

There is no doubt that the murder of Errington was a hugely popular act of revenge and was sanctioned by the Primitive Methodist Preachers who dominated the spiritual life of the Hetton community. For them, politics and religion were inseparable. God was on the side of the union. The union was God's instrument in his battle between good and evil.

Buddle complained in a letter to Londonderry that the leading preachers at Hetton frequently assembled the people from one hundred to four hundred together on the roadside and offered up prayers for the success of the strike and also that:

> The men who were brought from a distance, to work in a colliery, the blacklegs as they called them, might be injured, either lamed or killed; and they rejoiced when anything did happen to them.

And with direct reference to the shooting of Errington:

> The Ranter preachers are lauding this act 'the murder was the instrument in the hands of the Almighty, to inflict this judgment on the miscreant who betrayed the Union.'

If Buddle's account is correct, then the attitude of the Hetton preachers was in stark contrast to the public pronouncements of Hepburn who condemned these acts, appealing to the pitmen not to succumb to violence. But these preachers in Hetton were Hepburn's closest collaborators, men whom Robert Colls in his invaluable book, *The Pitmen of the Northern Coalfield,* calls Hepburn's cadre. It begs the question: was Hepburn so completely at odds with the philosophy of his cadre or were exhortations on the rostrum tactical rather than an expression of deeply held conviction?

If Hepburn's attitude towards violence had its contradictions, so did that of Major General Sir Henry Bouverie, commander of the King's army on the Northern coalfield. He was not very happy about getting involved in the messy business of civil disorder. He believed that his forces were not sufficient to suppress the pitmen should they resort to direct action and was well aware that he relied more on the miners' respect for the military than force at his command.

The pitmen's capacity to fight was soon to be tested on the southern banks of the Tyne at the village of Friars Goose. In May, after the evictions at Hetton had been completed, owners moved their army of candymen and special constables to evict the miners of Tyne Main colliery. When the eviction party arrived the miners retaliated using no more than their fists.

According to Fynes in his *History of the Northumberland and Durham Miners,* the trouble began when the ejection party arrived from the Hetton evictions under the supervision of a Mr Forsyth. Confronted by a large body of pitmen from Tyne Main colliery and their families, Forsyth issued the constables with two rounds of cartridges containing swan shot. This enraged the pitmen, who were also being goaded by the candymen as they manhandled the furniture out of the pitmen's cottages. The candymen,

. . . not content with bundling the furniture to the door as if it were rubbish, kept calling them cowards, aroused in the breasts of the men a very dangerous spirit.

The pitmen rushed the guard house which had been set up in one of the houses, overpowered the sentry and carried off the guns. The miners positioned themselves on the higher ground, trapping the constables in a narrow lane. From their vantage-point they pelted the constables with stones and brickbats. In retaliation the constables opened fire on the miners and rushed towards higher ground near the house of the viewer. The miners returned the fire, wounding several constables.

By this time Forsyth was badly wounded about the head and sent two constables to alert the military. The pitmen blocked their path and the messengers were forced to take evasive action. One finally succeeded, though severely wounded, to gallop through Newcastle to the barracks.

By the time the military arrived, accompanied by the mayor of Newcastle and the rector of Gateshead, the miners had dispersed. The soldiers began a search of the area and arbitrarily arrested forty men without any evidence that they had taken part in the disturbance. Two of these men were union delegates who had just returned from a delegate meeting and could not have been present at the time of the evictions. They were tied to a cart and badly beaten and were half dead when they arrived at Newcastle jail. They were committed for trial at the next Durham Assizes and taken to Durham Jail under escort of the cavalry.

It was quite clear that the owners were now intent on smashing the union by brute force and had no interest in reaching a compromise. Bouverie, however, was incensed by the tactics of the magistrates and their constables and complained that their actions could only invite retaliation. He complained that calling the military after the event ment that 'in a very short time [the troops would] become the laughing stock of the County'.

Bouverie was clearly unhappy in his role, caught in the cross-fire between the union and the owners. He was clear that the magistrates and owners enjoyed the same interests in the coal trade. He rejected the magistrates' protestations that the

Battle of Friars Goose 1832

pitmen were on the brink of insurrection and urged them to negotiate a settlement. Robert Branding, a leading coal owner and magistrate, flatly rejected Bouverie's advice on 12 June, declaring that it had to be 'a fight to the finish'.

Hepburn's tactic of allowing those men to work who could reach a settlement was now under pressure as it became necessary to increase the levy on their wages from 25 to 50 per cent. Under this arrangement the only way that more funds could be raised for the increasingly beleaguered strikers was to end the union's imposed limit on the amount of coal a union man could produce. While this increased earnings and proportionately the levy, it also undermined the strike by increasing the amount of coal in circulation. This tactic was frustrated by the owners' refusal to pay any more than the absolute minimum required by the bond.

The unbound men were by now reduced to a state of desperation. On 11 June, at 5 p.m., a South Shields magistrate, Nicholas Fairless, was on horseback riding to Jarrow colliery when he was accosted by two begging miners, Jobling and Armstrong. A fracas developed and Fairless was thrown from his horse and sustained a severe wound from which he died ten days later. Armstrong escaped but Jobling was arrested and taken to Durham Jail. He was brought to trial on 1 August, charged with murder.

Three days earlier on 8 July, a meeting of striking miners took place at Chirton, near North Shields. The meeting was disrupted by a group of special constables and a fight between constables and men ensued. A well respected miner, Cuthbert Skipsey from Percy Main colliery, intervened to calm the situation, when Constable George Weddle drew his pistol and shot Skipsey dead on the spot. He left a widow and six children. Weddle was arrested and charged with manslaughter and tried on 3 August.

At Jobling's trial he pleaded that he had not struck the blow that had wounded Fairless. When Fairless had fallen from his horse he had run from the scene. On looking back he had seen Armstrong standing over Fairless with a stick. Judge Parke decreed that, although Jobling did not strike the fatal blow, by being present he was equally guilty.

It took the jury just sixteen minutes to declare Jobling guilty of murder. He was sentenced to hang in public on 3 August. Parke was quite clear of the cause of the murder:

> It was the melancholy consequences of that combination amongst workmen which has prevailed in this county for so long a time. . . .

Combinations that are alike injurious to the public interest and to the interests of those persons concerned in them. . . . I trust in God that death will operate as it is intended to do, as a warning to all others, and deter them from following the example of your crime.

But hanging was not enough for the establishment. Gibbeting had been abolished in Britain in 1825. An Act of Parliament was rushed through which decreed that murderers would be hanged and their bodies hung at the scene of their crime. Jobling was the first to be subject to this grisly act.

On the day of his hanging the scaffold was protected by a hundred soldiers, half of them cavalry, just in case the miners attempted a rescue. According to Fynes' report he mounted the scaffold and asked to address the crowd but the power of speech eluded him. As the trapdoor dropped, someone in the crowed, thought to be Armstrong, shouted: 'Farewell Jobling'. Jobling turned his head, dislodging the knot under his jawbone and suffering strangulation for several painful minutes before he died.

His body was cut down and his clothes removed. The naked body was immersed in tar to preserve it, reclothed and placed in an iron harness.

On the same day, the trial of Constable Weddle,

Trial, Sentence,

AND

EXECUTION

of **WILLIAM JOBLING**, who was **Executed at Durham**, on Friday Morning, **August 3rd, 1832**, for the **Wilful Murder** of **NICHOLAS FAIRLESS**, Esq., late **Magistrate at South Shields**,

On Wednesday morning, August 1st, 1832, the trial of William

Jobling in iron cage - Bede Art Gallery, Jarrow

who had shot Cuthbert Skipsey, was taking place in Newcastle. After sixteen hours he was found guilty of manslaughter and sentenced to six months' imprisonment.

On 7 August, at 7p.m., Jobling's body was taken in a four-wheeled cart, escorted by a troop of Hussars and a company of infantry, out of Durham to Chester-le-Street, Picktree, Sludge Row, Portabello over Black Fell to White Mare Pool, and on to the turnpike road to South Shields. At Jarrow Slake, the scene of the crime, the gruesome iron harness with Jobling's body within was suspended from a 20-foot pole erected in the slake 100 yards beyond the high tide mark. There it hung, a grisly reminder to the miners of Durham and Northumberland of the close unity of state and coal owners.

On the night of 31 August the body disappeared. It was widely believed that Jobling's friends came by boat when the tide was in, cut down the body and buried it at sea. Armstrong was never caught and was thought to have escaped to America.

Hepburn and the union were now in deep trouble. To add to their misery, cholera broke out in the villages. Hepburn figured that the pitmen had one last chance an all-out strike. Buddle was of the opinion that an all-out stoppage would 'settle the matter, one way or other for twenty years or more'.

Hepburn held a delegate meeting at South Shields on 8 August 1832 and put forward a resolution for a total stoppage. However, he failed to convince the delegates, who voted to continue as they were for a further ten weeks.

By the end of August cholera had spread to all the villages. Demoralisation set in and men began to seek work wherever and on whatever terms they were offered. The owners had won. On 20 September Hepburn was forced to stand with his men at Hetton colliery and watch as the overmen picked out whom they wanted to engage. Hepburn and the union delegates were not, of course, among them.

That night, Mathias Dunn noted in his diary that he was of the opinion that the men still wanted a union and that he thought one would survive despite all that had happened.

On Christmas Day 1832, a thinly attended meeting on Shadons Hill agreed to dissolve the union. Hepburn was now cast into the abyss. The God he had put so much faith in had deserted him and he, in turn, lost his faith in that God.

Standing steam haulage engine at drift mine

Chapter 2

In 1832 the pitmen of Northumberland and Durham had suffered a crushing defeat. The union was smashed and its leaders 'sacrificed'. According to Fynes' account, Hepburn was reduced to selling tea round the pit villages.

The great man who had led the miners through their struggles in 1831 and 1832, now shabbily clad, no one to converse with, broken down in spirits, proscribed and hunted, had to go and beg at Felling for employment.

Notwithstanding Fynes' sad description, Hepburn's political life was far from over. Hepburn and some of his comrades who led the 1832 strike were agitating at Wallsend colliery in 1835 in the aftermath of the Wallsend explosion where 109 men were killed on 18 June of that year.

It is likely that trade unionism was not completely dead but retreated to more isolated and loose organisations based on individual pits. Union stalwarts like Ben Embleton did not give up their dream of a new county-wide union and trudged from village to village preaching to whoever dared to listen, extolling the virtues of trade unionism and the need to build a new county union.

But the coal trade was growing and new collieries were being sunk throughout the county. The success of Hetton colliery in breaching the treacherous waters of the Sand Feeder and reaching the rich coal measures below the limestone had encouraged the sinking of even deeper shafts. Eppleton and Ellemore collieries were sunk at Hetton-le-Hole and Easington Lane in 1825. South Hetton in 1831, Pemberton colliery Monkwearmouth 1835 and Murton 1838. These pits were massive operations funded by joint stock companies, often with capital raised from outside the coalfield. This influx of capital created an expansion in the supply of coal and a shortage of labour.

On 28 January 1834 John Gully, a former prize fighter and one of Durham's more colourful mine owners, sank Thornley colliery. Green labour was recruited from as far afield as Cornwall, Lincolnshire and Ireland to work the pit and there is no doubt that many of the sacrificed men from 1832 changed their names and sought employment at this new winning.

Gully appointed Richard Heckles, a distinguished mining engineer, as the viewer of the new colliery. He was also a 'distinguished' opponent of trade unionism.

England and its emerging working class was in a state of unrest. The passions of the Reform movement and the memories of Peterloo were reawakening. The great Reform Bill of 1832, which Hepburn and his followers had welcomed so enthusiastically at their meeting on Boldon Fell in August 1831, had failed to change the lot of the lower classes. It extended the right to vote to some sections of the middle classes but left the lower orders in the same position as they had always been: bereft of rights and economically destitute. This gave impetus to the rise of the Chartist movement which demanded manhood suffrage, secret ballots, payment for MPs, the abolition of the property qualification for MPs, equal electoral districts and annual parliaments.

The Chartist movement, like the reform movement which preceded it, was diverse, drawing its followers from all sections of the

Pemberton Main colliery, Monkwearmouth - T H Hair

middle and working classes. As it developed momentum it divided into two wings, those who favoured the use of force, the Physical Force Chartists and those who favoured the force of argument and reason, the Moral Force Chartists. The Physical Force Chartists dominated in the North East of England and were often seen at rallies carrying banners with the motto, 'he that hath no sword let him sell his shirt and buy one'.

The village of Winlaton in the north of the county and the village of Thornley to the south both became centres of Chartist movement. Winlaton was known to be armed with both rifle and cannon and at Thornley Pit the blacksmiths made pikes

and 'calthropes' iron spikes linked together and used as a defence against a cavalry charge.

Tommy Hepburn was an active leader in this movement. On Christmas Day 1838 the Northern Political Union held a meeting on 'The Fourth', where Newcastle Central Station stands today, to elect delegates to the Chartist Convention. John Julian Harney, one of the delegates elected that day, recalled fifty years later, in an article in the *Newcastle Weekly Chronicle,* that:

> Ralph Curry nominated Dr John Taylor as one of the three delegates. Thomas Hepburn seconded the motion. Tommy Hepburn, as he was familiarly termed, was of middle age,

large and somewhat heavy of look, but an intelligent, energetic leader of the miners.

This description of Hepburn in 1839 tends to contradict the image of a broken man shunned by his fellow miners.

On 20 April 1839 the Chartists called a meeting on the Town Moor. They met to discuss what action they should resort to if the Charter was rejected by parliament. Tommy Hepburn chaired the meeting. In an attempt to prevent the meeting taking place the city authorities read the Riot Act

three times. In an act of defiance, Tommy Hepburn stood up and declared: 'John Fife, mayor of Newcastle, I tell you that your proclamation is no law. You have no right to prevent us holding our meetings.'

Eyewitnesses reported that Hepburn's bold defiance did much to inspire the meeting.

Chartist agitation reached a peak in 1839 and the Physical Force wing was calling for an end to the government of the rich and a radical redistribution of wealth. The movement was by no means exclusively male. Female political unions were formed in many villages and women convened many meetings in the pit villages to agitate for fundamental change and the use of force if necessary.

In July 1839 the arrest of Dr Taylor, John Julian Harney and other Chartist leaders caused a wave of strikes throughout the region and the Thornley men laid the pit idle and commandeered a locomotive on the Durham-to-Sunderland railway which they drove to Sunderland to attend a protest meeting. The colliery remained closed for a week and on 13 July a massive rally was held at Fatfield where pikes were openly exchanged on the field. The Thornley men were only persuaded to return to work when a company of the 98th Regiment of Foot arrived in the village.

Martin Jude

On 15 January 1842 the Thornley miners placed an advertisement in the Chartist paper, *The Northern Star*, calling for a meeting on 22 January 'to adopt measures for resistance to the coal owners and their viewers'. The advertisement was signed by Thomas Birrell 'by order of the Thornley Colliery Union'.

The chairman of the meeting was Ben Embleton from Wingate and although the attendance at this meeting was sparse it did elect Thomas Hall of Thornley to convene a further meeting the next month at Monkwearmouth.

The new Northumberland and Durham Miners' Association soon became well established and united with other county unions throughout Britain and Ireland in the first national union of mineworkers, which was called the Miners' Association of Great Britain and Ireland. Its first meeting was held on 7 November 1842 in Wakefield, West Yorkshire. One of its first actions was to appoint a young lawyer, William Prowting Roberts, as its legal representative.

Roberts was born in 1806, the son of a vicar of Chelmsford in Essex. He was educated at Charterhouse public school, trained as a solicitor and first practised in Bath. There could not have been a greater contrast between his privileged early life and that of the northern pitmen. As a

W P Roberts

young man he first supported the Tories. It was the treatment of agricultural labourers in Wiltshire in the aftermath of the Captain Swing riots of 1831-2 that converted him to the cause of the working classes.

Farm labourers rose up against the introduction of steam-driven threshing machines which were the cause of high levels of seasonal unemployment. When their demands were not met these half starving men resorted to violence and burned down hayricks and destroyed threshing machines. The government retaliated with devastating consequence and nineteen labourers were executed, fifty transported and six hundred and forty-four imprisoned. Roberts was a deeply religious man. It is thought that this treatment of men who had been driven to acts of desperation turned him from a middle-class solicitor into a radical champion of the cause of labour.

On 24 November the Thornley miners, with the support of the new union, struck work when the viewer Heckles enforced the terms of the bond to such a degree that hewers were being fined amounts greater in some cases than their earnings. Heckles' weighing machine was unstamped, which was against the terms of the bond, but this did not deter him from prosecuting his hewers for striking. Warrants were duly issued for the arrest of sixty-eight men, all of whom were active in the union.

Roberts led a brilliant defence but the magistrates were unmoved and convicted them of a breach of the Masters' and Servants' Act and gave them a six-month jail sentence. Roberts immediately left for London and returned with a High Court writ of habeas corpus. The men were taken to the High Court and acquitted.

For a court to find in the favour of ordinary working men was unheard of and the Thornley victory must have sent shock waves through the ranks of the coalowners.

On 2 March 1844, twenty thousand pitmen met on Shadons Hill and agreed that they would not bind themselves until after the national conference due to be held in Glasgow on 25 March. The National Miners' Association was growing in confidence but did not as yet represent all the miners in Britain. The decision to hold its conference in Glasgow was an attempt to persuade more miners to join from areas of Scotland where membership of the union was sparse.

Representatives of seventy thousand miners attended the Glasgow conference. The delegates from Durham and Northumberland, invigorated by the union's success at Thornley, pressed the conference to call a national strike to address their grievances, but were narrowly defeated.

Martin Jude, treasurer of the Northumberland and Durham union, agreed with the conference and urged the delegates to be more cautious. But Ben Embleton, from Wingate, appealed to the conference, saying that he knew as much of the miners of Northumberland and Durham as any man. He fully believed that if they were allowed to fight their own battle and keep other men [miners from the other coalfields] from filling their places, they would come off victorious.

Embleton won the day and permission was granted for Durham and Northumberland to

Seaham Docks 1900   *Photo: Easington Past and Present*

proceed alone, with the assistance of the National Miners' Association.

When the delegates return from Glasgow, Roberts drew up the terms of a bond which would be acceptable to the pitmen and a meeting was called on Shadons Hill. Over twenty thousand miners marched to the meeting, behind bands and banners. Spirits were high and the men in no mood for compromise.

The chairman of the new union was Mark Dent, who told the meeting that he was confident that if the men stood together and resisted the terms of the masters' bond they would get their just rewards. Speakers John Tulip and Edward Richardson, who were delegates, and William Daniels, editor of the *Miners Advocate*, all stressed the need for the men to remain calm and keep the law. The meeting resolved never to agree to the terms of the owners' bond but to announce their willingness to meet the employers to resolve the matter.

This was the first truly universal strike in the history of the Northumberland and Durham miners. In 1831 and 1832 collieries had been allowed to settle with those owners who came to an agreement and working miners had been levied to support those still out on strike. Now all collieries were out and agreed not to return until all had settled. This all-or-nothing strategy was a big risk as the new union had few resources to alleviate the hardship.

Despite the advice of the leaders, violence did break out in the first weeks of the strike. At South Hetton twenty hewers and deputies had bound themselves before the strike began. On the night of 5 April their houses were attacked and the windows smashed.

A more serious situation arose at Kelloe colliery five days later. A group of men were filling waggons with coal when they were attacked and 'severely maimed' by a gang of miners from Cassop and Pattner's colliery. One newspaper report described how the overman, Mr Brydon, supplied the blacklegs with pistols and warned the union men that he would shoot anyone who came near to them. When he was hit by a stone in the face he fired into the crowd, seriously wounding William Hodgson and provoking a riot. Finally the military were called and the rioters were captured and charged.

Although serious, these disturbances were not widespread. George Hunter, one of Lord Londonderry's viewers, was intrigued to see his miners 'working peacefully in their gardens, which they never did in 1832'. He wondered: 'What does it all mean?'

Londonderry and the Hetton coal company had reasonably good stocks of coal. The shortage of coal caused by the strike resulted in escalating prices. By slowly releasing coal from their stocks on to the market, they were able to make a small killing. Other owners were not as lucky.

Hunter was positively in favour of a short strike and wrote: 'It would be bad for us if the strike was not to go on for a month or six weeks.'

There was clearly a division between those owners who had high stocks of unsold coal and those who had none. When the coal owners' committee met on 12 April, some of the more desperate proprietors argued for turning the families out of their homes but Hunter did not press the matter, as he latter disclosed: 'We had an object to gain . . . to keep them quiet until we got our old coals away.'

Londonderry was still viewed with suspicion by other owners who remembered the way he had broken ranks and settled in 1831. The miners may well have also hoped that Londonderry would prove the weak link again.

At the beginning of the strike Londonderry was in Paris but returned to London. Hunter wrote to him on 23 April: 'The men are all quiet, and from what I hear they are calculating upon you coming home, when they could get what they want and go back to work again.' He advised Londonderry to keep away from the coalfield.

The miners' leaders persisted in the view that the best way to win their demands was to keep the peace and win public support. They embarked on a number of public meetings to argue their case, and succeeded in getting the support of other unions.

By 11 May, Londonderry's coal stocks were all but depleted. Until now he had followed Hunter's advice and resisted evicting the pitmen from their houses while he had stocks to sell on the London market. Returning from London, he held a meeting with the pitmen from his collieries on 28 May at Penshaw. Far from settling with the men, he issued them with a stark warning: 'Either

return to work or make way for those who will.'

By the end of May he began to evict miners and their families from his collieries in Pittington and Rainton and introduced Irish labour from his estates in the north of Ireland.

The union was still confident and the pitmen solid. They continued the propaganda campaign, taking it to London. On 13 June they held a meeting in London which was chaired by TS Duncombe, the

Engine near Pittingdon - T H Hair

Member of Parliament for the Borough of Finsbury and a champion of the miners' cause. The Chartist leader Feargus O'Connor was present and the meeting concluded by passing a resolution calling for parliament to 'sort out the trouble at its root'.

Throughout the first to weeks of June more blacklegs were introduced into the area from Wales, Staffordshire, Cornwall and Ireland and more pitmen and their families were evicted. Across the county, along the hedgerows and on the moors, small tented villages were appearing daily, constructed from furniture: sheets and canvas were the only protection from the elements.

Londonderry was single-minded in pursuit of his own self-interest. By releasing his coal on to the market in the early days of the strike he had broken the rules of the vend and exceeded his quota, but had argued that the vend could not operate as others had nothing to vend. Now he was losing money as the sanding costs of his collieries had to be paid. On 19 June, he suggested to the coal committee that they concede to the pitmen the yearly bond, with the proviso that if there was any breach of the terms the bond could be terminated. This act of breathtaking opportunism was dismissed by the other owners.

Londonderry's accountant, Hindhaugh, wrote four days later: 'Now the stocks of coal are gone the collieries would be dependent on the banks.'

The introduction of raw labour into the collieries did not run smoothly. Hewing coal is a developed skill and it takes time to develop both skill and strength. When the extravagant promises of high wages did not materialise, many of the strangers resorted to strike action themselves and in one case a group of Cornishmen in Northumberland absconded and a reward of £50 was advertised for their capture.

At the beginning of July spirits were high, despite the obvious hardship. The Ranter Preachers of the Primitive Chapels were playing their part in providing the miners with the ideological fuel to sustain the dispute. They organised prayer meetings where, according to Tremenheere, 'prayers were publicly offered up for the successful result of the strike' and men went to these meetings 'to get their faith strengthened' and 'to encourage each other in the confidence that the strike would succeed'.

But it was not to be. Although the strike remained relatively solid until the end of July, hardship and the continuous introduction of blacklegs into the coalfield gradually sapped the will of the men to continue.

On 13 August two hundred and forty families arrived from Flintshire and were settled throughout the Hetton and Lambton collieries. In the first two weeks of August over a thousand union men returned to work, mainly in Durham. This was the watershed of the strike and, despite mass meetings in Newcastle and Durham, there was a general return to work. The pitmen of the Tyne and those in Northumberland hung on, but by the end of August it was all over.

Once the men returned to work they wrought their bitterness and disappointment out on the strangers who had been brought into the area. On 11 August, the breaksman at Ravensworth colliery was found shot dead. In Northumberland the Welsh blacklegs received such harsh treatment that they packed up and returned to Wales. Only one remained, the one who had been instrumental in bringing them there. He preferred to endure the hostility of the Northumberland pitmen than that of his fellow Welshmen.

Labour was disunited, but all was not well between the owners of capital. During the strike Londonderry and others had greatly exceeded their share of the vend. When the Coal Committee insisted that they pay £49,973 in compensation to the owners who had not, they refused. Even when this figure was reduced to £29,874 they remained adamant.

A crake man, the union equivalent of the town crier

On 3 May 1845 the practice of limiting the supply of coal to London came to an end.

A mid-nineteenth century four-ton chaldron wagon

Haswell Colliery circa 1880s

Chapter 3

The 1844 strike ended with the pitmen forced to accept owners' terms and the introduction of a new monthly bond. The union had sustained a near-fatal blow, but the Durham and Northumberland Miners' Association did not immediately collapse, although it was greatly weakened and denuded of members. As ever, the leaders were victimised and many forced to leave the county and seek work in other coalfields. Many suffered both the oppression of the masters and the criticism of the men.

The collieries had been working only a few weeks when a terrible explosion occurred at Haswell colliery, killing ninety-five men and boys. WP Roberts made strenuous efforts at the inquest to show that the colliery viewer's neglect was responsible for the huge loss of life, but the coroner put every obstacle in his path and the tragedy was deemed by the jury to be an accident.

In the aftermath of this terrible tragedy Martin Jude turned his attention to parliament and mounted a campaign for legislation to force mineowners to adopt safer working practices. TS Duncombe MP, who had championed the miners' cause throughout the 1844 strike, collaborated closely with Jude to this end. Although Jude had not been in favour of the strike he had worked tirelessly for its success and was well respected by miners.

Throughout 1847 Jude and Duncombe fought to get legalisation passed through parliament on a wide range of issues affecting the lives of miners. They concentrated on the need for improved ventilation, the abolition of gunpowder underground, and the elimination of the truck system, always to be defeated by the vested interest of the mineowners.

For years the truck system had been one of the greatest causes of discontent in the coalfields. The owners or their close relatives ran truck shops, or 'tommy shops', as they were known in the north. At these shops the masters sold inferior food and equipment at above the market price. Miners had no choice but to buy their provisions at these stores and when a miner was laid off or had his wages reduced by fines, goods would be sold on credit. Many pitmen found that they were continuously in debt. Since this debt was deducted from the miners' wage at source, in reality they were being paid not in coin but in kind. If a miner was in

Haswell miners 1860s

debt to the company store at the time of the annual binding it was impossible for him to leave the colliery. By this system indentured labour was in fact reduced to slavery.

'Tommy shops' were one of the main reasons for the emergence of the cooperative movement which was to flourish in the villages of Northumberland and Durham in the latter half of the nineteenth century.

By 1847 the union was on its last legs. As the coal trade plummeted into depression, conditions in the mining communities became more and more miserable.

A final blow was struck against the cause of working-class emancipation in 1848 when the Great Charter bearing the signatures of over 4 million people was presented to parliament and rejected. Sporadic and disorganised uprisings took place across the country. Government spies and agents made it difficult to separate genuine insurrections from the handiwork of the provocateur. In the summer and autumn of 1848 a reign of terror was unleashed. Chartists were arrested, often dragged from their beds in the early hours. Roberts did his best to defend those who were charged with sedition, constantly moving from one town to the next. But there were too many even for a man as energetic as Roberts.

The defeat of Chartism had its effect in the ranks of the National Miners' Association. Riven with internal conflict, it had all but collapsed by the end of 1849. Unionism in Durham was again reduced to clandestine meetings on the moors or in back alleys, anywhere away from the watchful eye of the owners and their agents.

For a brief moment in March 1849 it looked as if the union was to be revived when a wave of strikes swept through South Northumberland. Cholera, not for the first time, came to the aid of the masters and the strike movement was snuffed out as quickly as it arose. It was to be another nine years before a degree of confidence was restored and Jude and others began to look to the establishment of a county union.

On 18 September 1858, a mass meeting was held at Black Fell, organised by Martin Jude for the purpose of establishing a county union. Present at this meeting was a Scottish miners' leader called Alexander MacDonald. MacDonald had started work as a miner at the age of eight. Through his own efforts he educated himself and, by the time he was twenty-five, gained a place at Glasgow university. He supported himself by working in the pits in the holidays and finally qualified as a school teacher. By saving and investing his money in mining stock he became a man of independent means and counted one of the biggest mineowners in Scotland as his friend. As a wealthy man he was able to devote his time to the building of new National Miners' Association. The union that MacDonald envisaged, however, was quite different from that which had been built in the age of Chartism. MacDonald wanted a loose association of county unions which did not fight for better wages but acted as a pressure group to encourage parliament to pass legislation regulating the conditions and safety.

Roberts, who also addressed the meeting on Black Fell, represented the old school of thought. Despite the demise of Chartism, he remained true to his old beliefs. Roberts was unique: he was from the middle class yet he was a Physical Force Chartist, not averse to holding up a pistol at meetings to hammer home a point. He was a legal representative for Karl Marx and Friedrich Engels, but did not share their socialist views. While most unionists were either atheists or non-conformist he remained a member of the established Church of England. One thing was clear: MacDonald's 'New Realism' and Roberts 'Chartism' did not rest easily together.

When a new National Miners' Association was formed on 9 November 1859, Roberts was invited to become its legal officer on a salary of £800 per annum.

In 1860 the tireless work of Martin Jude came to

fruition when parliament passed the Mines Act which governed the safety and inspection of mines, placed restrictions on the employment of child labour, and made provision for the election of checkweighmen. This last concession was to have a profound effect on the development of trade unions: those who drew up the legislation no doubt thought it would eliminate disputes. However, the need to hold elections for the position of checkweighman involved a degree of organisation, and once elected the checkweighman became a representative of the workforce. It was but a small step from representative to leader. Checkweighmen soon became the equivalent of full-time union officials. From 1861, when the Mines Act became law, colliery-based unions developed throughout county Durham around the annual election of checkweighmen. In choosing one of their community who could be trusted, Durham pitmen invariably chose a Primitive Methodist.

Martin Jude never lived to see the effects of the Bill for which he fought so hard: he died a pauper in August 1860 in South Shields and was buried in Elswick cemetery, Newcastle. His tenacity had kept the flame of trade unionism burning and paved the way for a more enlightened era.

The 1860 Act gave Roberts a new raft of legal rights on which he could fight and press the

Murton colliery circa 1880s

advantage home. His strategy had always rested on a two-pronged attack: while he mounted a legal defence of workers in court, he would encourage direct action through strikes and demonstrations.

On 9 December 1863 the national council of the miners' union passed a resolution repudiating strikes. Within weeks Roberts was locked in struggle with a mine owner of a South Wales colliery which resulted in an unofficial strike. MacDonald and his national committee were incensed.

Roberts was accused of feathering his own nest at the expense of the union, a clear slander which Roberts vehemently denied. However, MacDonald and his supporters succeeded in removing him from his position as the legal officer in the national union. Roberts was forced to engage in a campaign to defend his good name and this controversy and growing discontent at MacDonald's style of leadership split the new miners' association.

In 1863 the owners in Northumberland and Durham announced that they intended ending the monthly bond introduced after the 1844 strike and replacing it with a yearly bond. This threat created a wave of opposition in Northumberland and led to the formation of The Northumberland and Durham Miners' Mutual Confident Association with the object of restricting the hours of labour and reducing death in the mines. The Primitive Methodist, William Crawford, was elected as the secretary of this new organisation which, at its onset, represented 3,500 men but quickly grew in strength. During 1863 meetings were convened throughout the two counties and many thousands of miners were recruited. The reintroduction of the yearly bond and the persistently low hewing prices fuelled the desire to build a new union.

The pitmen of the Great Northern Coalfield had been without an effective union for almost two decades and as soon as a new union was built they lost no time in taking action to have their grievances addressed. Before the union could consolidate support and build up a war-chest, action was being taken all over the county, the most famous of which was the 'rocking strike' at the collieries owned by the Joseph Love in the Crook area.

Love was unique amongst coal owners, having been a pitman himself. He was a New Connexion Methodist and had been instrumental in building chapels and funding schools for the communities which worked his mines. This paternalism was by not uncommon for mine owners in Durham; neither was their recourse to brutal measures when their interests were threatened.

Miners in Love's collieries were paid by volume and not by weight. As the tubs of coal trundled their way to bank, the coal settled and often the level of a full tub underground was below the rim of the tub when it emerged at bank. These tubs were deemed to be of short measure and not only were the hewers not paid for the coal, they were also fined. The weighmen received a commission from Love for every tub they disqualified.

To avoid a fine, the hewers were forced to rock the tubs at the coal face to settle the coal before it was despatched to bank. This arduous and time-

Haraton colliery 1880s

consuming task was a further burden to an already badly-used body of men. On 16 October, one thousand two hundred men at Love's collieries took strike action. Love brutally turned women and children out of their tied cottages in appalling weather conditions and introduced blacklegs to replace the striking miners. His actions were so harsh that he was condemned in the local press, not noted for its support for miners or their unions.

This strike wave put an impossible strain on the union. When strike funds were not forthcoming, disagreements and disunity prevailed. The Northumberland miners became so disillusioned by the 'anarchy' that prevailed in Durham that early in 1865 they split from Durham. Being in union with Durham was likened to 'being connected to a body of death'.

The late 1860s saw fundamental changes in the trade union movement. Unions outside the mining industry were becoming more stable and in 1868 the Trades Union Congress was formed.

In Durham Roberts fought one final battle that was decisive in the establishment of a permanent union. The viewer of Wearmouth colliery was Richard Heckles, Roberts' old adversary from Thornley colliery.

In March 1869 the hewers at Wearmouth colliery were told that, due to the state of the coal trade, hewing prices were to be reduced from those of the previous year. The men bound, but by May found that they could not make a living and broke the terms of the bond by going on strike.

After a week Heckles issued notes for the men to be given a quart of beer each if they returned to work. The men returned the notes with the terse observation that the time had passed when men could be bought with a jug of ale, adding that beef and bread may have produced a different reply.

Heckles then returned to his tactic of 1843 and prosecuted four of the men under the Masters' and Servants' Act. Roberts was engaged to defend them and when Heckles came to the witness box Roberts rose and enquired: 'Mr Heckles, don't I know you?'

The court exploded in laughter.

Roberts challenged Heckles to prove that the men had actually had the bond read to them, or that men who had put their mark to the bond had actually signed the document. He resorted to the tactics he had used to defend the Thornley men and produced a succession of miners who stated that they would rather go to prison than continue to work under the terms of the bond.

After an adjournment that lasted two weeks the magistrates declared the strike illegal and the owners refused to grant a wage increase.

What followed was an incredible display of solidarity. The men agreed to vacate their cottages and resign their jobs. They marched as one body of men to the colliery offices and handed in their lamps and their colliery rule books. So affected were the deputies who had remained at work that they too joined the strike. Without deputies, the very fabric of the mine was at risk and Heckles, arch-opponent of organised labour, was forced to capitulate and offer to waive the bond, leaving the question of wages to arbitration.

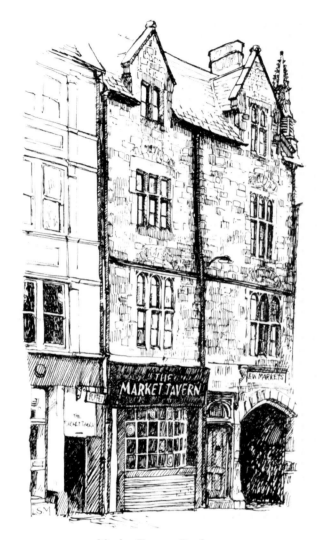

Market Tavern, Durham

On Saturday, 20 November 1869, a meeting of delegates in the Market Tavern in Durham Market Square met and established Durham Miners' Mutual Association, a union which was to endure.

This new union came to life at a fortunate period of history: Durham coal was entering an unprecedented period of prosperity. The Franco-Prussian war in 1870 paralysed the coalfields of Alsace and Lorraine and the mine owners of Durham were busily taking advantage of the rising price of coal stimulated by the disruption of supplies from Europe. Such was the disruption that by 1872 Durham coal had everything going for it: high prices and rising demand.

Shafts were being sunk to Durham's seams as fast as sinkers could be found to sink them; *The Victorian County History* gives us an insight into the extent of the development.

In the year of 1872 :

No. 2 shaft, Florence pit, Kepier colliery, was sunk from the surface to the Busty seam.

The Pelton New Winning, Newfield, was commenced and sunk from the surface to the Busty seam.

Cowen's pit, Blaydon Burn colliery, was sunk from the surface to the Brockwell Seam.

Witton pit, Charlaw colliery, was sunk from the Hutton to the Busty Seam.

No. 1 shaft, Chilton colliery was commenced on 29 February, and sunk to the Main coal seam.

A series of borings was put down from the surface on the Holmside Royalty, proving the

Hutton Seam and upper coals, and another series of boreholes in the vicinity of Woodlands colliery, proving the Brockwell Seam.

Boring operations from the surface were also in progress in the vicinity of Crake Scar colliery, Cockfield, and others by Coulson on the Winston estate, proving a coal seam 30in thick, lying just above the Gannister Beds.

Commenced to sink the New Pit, Trimdon Grange Colliery, from the surface to the Busty seam.

East Howle Colliery commenced to sink and was put down to the Brockwell Seam.

In this year there were seventeen Guibal ventilators at work in South Durham alone. Air compressing plant was erected at Ryhope and at North Hetton Collieries for working underground , machinery, coal cutters etc.

Great advances had been made in mining technique. Steel could now be manufactured in great quantities by the new Bessemer converters. Central to this process was the manufacture of coke, increasing further the demand for good coking coal. The collieries of Durham, the laboratories of machine innovation, were themselves the greatest beneficiaries of this powerful new material. Stronger and more efficient steam engines could be built, powering better pumps and more efficient fans. Although the pick was to last in most pits well into the twentieth century, compressors were being developed to power pneumatic cutting machines.

This was the period of electromagnetism which transformed Michael Faraday's laboratory experiment linking the new phenomenon, electricity, to mechanical movement and produced, in time, the electric motor. By the turn of the century the mining engineer would be able to transmit power down the mine by cable to huge haulage motors.

While machinery was developing apace, painfully slow progress was being made in the field of mining safety. After the horrendous disaster at New Hartley Hester colliery in 1862, where two hundred and four men and boys perished for want of a second means of egress, public opinion prevailed and a Bill was passed in parliament requiring two shafts at all new mines. Furnace ventilation had reduced the instances of explosion and remained the principal method of ventilation throughout the nineteenth century. But disasters still occurred all too frequently and the almost daily carnage due to roof falls continued as production was traded for safety.

The new pitmen's union was making steady progress. Old Tommy Ramsay, hero of the 1844 strike, had come in from the cold. This faithful unionist, who had trudged from village to village, crake in hand, expounding the cause of unionism, sleeping under hedgerows, shunned by miners fearful of the consequences of being seen in his company, was now given a job as a union agent, and a salary to go with it.

This new union was led by Primitive Methodists, men with missionary zeal. For them, not to be a member of the union was to deny the

Early pneumatic cutter

will of God; it was a sin. This new union was carving out its place at the centre of Durham village life, a place it held unrivalled for more than a hundred years.

These men believed that if the union was strong, then the leaders were strong and the employers would listen to reason, and reason would prevail. For Crawford, Foreman and Patterson, Capital and Labour were two noble beasts, each having their place. If they were in conflict with each other then a lesser beast, the consumer, would take advantage. If they sat down and reasoned together both would benefit. This was their fervent belief.

The mine owners of Durham had never recognised

a union amongst pitmen. Their response to strikes in the past had been violent, relying on brute force. But in 1872 they had much to lose and so formed themselves into the North of England United Coal Trades Association, and decided to give reason a chance.

When this new association invited the DMA to the negotiating table in 1872, there was no hesitation. The first meeting took place in February of that year and the union requested an advance in wages of 35 per cent for all men working underground; 20 per cent was granted. Later that year the owners agreed that the hated yearly bond, that had kept the pitmen of Durham in a state of semi-serfdom, would be abolished.

The Durham miner was now a free man to sell his labour where he chose.

The new miners' union was not without its internal problems. The DMA leaders favoured a centralised union based on full-time agents. They far preferred to be given the power to negotiate with the employers and to reach a settlement without further consultation with the ordinary miner. If the paternalism of the employer was expressed in the occasional feast when opening a new mine, the building of a church or school, or just the owner's wife playing Lady Bountiful around the village, then the union leaders had their own brand of paternalism, the paternalism of a Father who knows what's best for his children.

The DMA, however, had grown out of local associations based on particular collieries; the economic life of the village centred on the pit. The local lodge of the union was the only means through which all the frustrations of day-to-day life could be resolved. These village communities exercised a gravitational pull away from the centre, preventing lodges from becoming satellites of the Durham leadership. They had their own orbit around the various communities they represented.

This antagonism between the DMA leaders and the miners they represented erupted into open revolt the moment the trade took a downturn. The coincidence of interest created between owners and men by the Franco-Prussian war and the disruption of European coal supplies was short-lived. It was one thing to allow the leaders to negotiate advances in a rising market; it was something else to allow them to negotiate reductions.

In April 1874 the owners demanded a reduction in wages of 25 per cent and the Durham leadership recommended that the union offer a reduction of 10 per cent. A coalfield conference accepted the recommendation, but when the decision was conveyed to the men they were incensed.

J Wilson, himself one of the Durham leaders, in his *History of the Durham Miners Association* recorded:

> The spirit of revolt was rampant throughout the county amongst the members of the Miners' Association. Circulars were sent out by District Councils, in which the Executive Committee was held to ridicule.

Mass meetings were held throughout the county. In some cases as many as ten thousand gathered to reject the offer and condemn the leadership, but on this occasion the Durham leaders finally prevailed and after a week of sporadic strikes a reduction of 10 per cent was narrowly agreed.

Five years later, in 1879, it was a different story. After a series of reductions the owners demanded a further 20-per-cent reduction. To reach an agreement the executive asked for 'full and uncontrolled power', but were denied this by the membership. The newly formed Federation Board, representing Miners, Enginemen and Deputies, offered 7.5 per cent and the owners replied with an offer of a 10-per-cent reduction underground and 7.5 per cent at bank. The Board recommended acceptance of this new offer. John Wilson again recorded the response:

There arose fierce agitation in the county and on every hand mass meetings were held protesting against the terms. As is the case in matters of this kind, orators vehement if not polished sprang up from every quarter, whose stock-in-trade consisted of foul epithets which they hurled at the Committee and Federation Board. So desperate was the situation that certain of the Committee were in fear and came into public view as little as possible.

Evicting miners families from their houses

Wilson, explains how he was affected by this dissent. As Chairman of the Wheatley Hill Lodge, he marched to a mass meeting held on the Sands at Durham. As they marched on to the field the first words that were heard were: 'There's one of the .....!, Let's put him in the river!'

The crowd surged towards him and there was a great struggle. When it was at its height a large miner fell on to the big drum of the brass band, which ruptured with an enormous bang. The cry went up: 'They are firing on us!'

Panic set in and the crowd stampeded for cover, leaving Wilson dishevelled, but unharmed.

The miners and their union were now in a familiar situation. The coal trade was at the bottom of a trough and the owners were in a strong position, and they knew it. The miners demanded arbitration but the owners refused, threatening to lock out all men who would not work for an increased reduction of 15 per cent. Again the Executive advised caution but the membership were adamant, and voted to strike. They finally returned to work seven weeks later on a reduction of eight-and-three-quarters per cent. A further one-and-a-quarter per cent reduction was added in July by arbitration.

Between 1873 and 1879 the Mechanics, Enginemen and Cokemen formed themselves into separate autonomous unions but in 1879 united with the DMA in the Durham Miners' Federation Board, which became the negotiating body in the county. Despite the many rebuffs from both men and management, the leaders of the DMA never tired in their quest for the elusive peace between men and masters. For a full twelve years they attempted to regulate wages by tying advances and reductions to the fluctuating price of coal, a system known as the sliding-scale, but it always broke down in the end. Reason could never overcome the simple fact that the owners' desire to defend profits was equal to the pitmen's desire to defend wages. The owners could not control the market and the Durham leaders could not control the men.

The union's activity was not confined to the question of wages. In 1890, in a rising market, they turned to the question of hours of work and secured an agreement restricting a hewer's shift to not more than seven hours, bank to bank. They also secured the agreement that no colliery would raise coals for more than ten hours per day, or eleven at some collieries. Although other underground classes of men continued to work ten hours this was an astounding success for hewers, jealously guarded over the years, though not without its problems.

Since the hewers represented the most numerous and influential section of the union, the union was obliged to continue their opposition to the struggle for a legal eight-hour day in fear that if it became law the owners would increase the hours of work for hewers. A further problem arose in that if the men working ten hours were reduced to eight, it would mean introducing a further shift and the subsequent drawing of coals for longer than ten hours. But they were at pains to explain that they were not opposing other classes of workmen achieving an eight-hour day: they believed this should be achieved by trade union activity and not by legislation.

This question of hours was the principal reason why, apart from a brief spell between 1892 an 1893, the DMA remained outside the Miners' Federation of Great Britain (MFGB) until 1908. The MFGB was formed in 1889 at a conference

Miners leaders 1890 - Alex MacDonald in centre, to his left John Wilson

in Newport and sought to unite miners both nationally and internationally to fight for higher wages and the legal eight-hour day.

The DMA leaders were opposed to the militant stance of this federation and its campaign for a legal eight-hour day, and remained members of the Miners' National Union, formed in 1863.

By 1892 the National Miners' Union represented only Northumberland and Durham. But during the Durham strike of 1892, which lasted 12 weeks and ended with the miners sustaining a 10-per-cent reduction in wages, the MFGB assisted the Durham miners financially, and the miners voted to join the MFGB, much to the leaders' displeasure.

In 1893, when the MFGB called a strike in defence of wages, the Durham leaders refused to support them and their membership fees were returned.

Scotland, South Wales and Durham took no part in the strike, which lasted sixteen weeks and was the first time miners in different coalfields had taken action together, with a powerful effect on the economy of the country.

An explosion at West Stanley colliery on
16 February 1909 claimed the lives of
168 men and boys. Frank Keegan, the
miners local inspector was acclaimed a
hero for his part in rescuing 26 men.

Frank Keegan, grandfather of Kevin Keegan

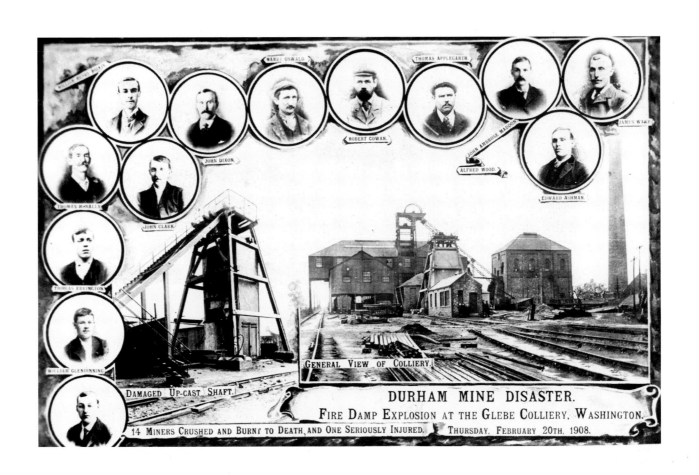

*On 20 February 1908, 14 miners were crushed and burned to death and
one seriously injured in an explosion at the Glebe colliery, Washington*

Sinking Ryhope colliery 1852

Chapter 4

By the dawn of the twentieth century Durham miners were truly a force to be reckoned with: not only in numbers and organisation but, more and more, in their fighting capacity and ideas. There were 31,000 miners in the DMA in 1872, but by 1898 membership was 69,132; by 1903 it was 86,346; and by 1910 it had reached 121,805.

The Durham coalfield was entering its final phase of development. Production peaked in 1913 when 166,000 men were employed in the industry in the county of Durham.

The technique of freezing the area around a new sinking enabled coal companies to sink shafts through the limestone that concealed the coal measures in the east of the coalfield. The Herculean struggle against the waters of the Sand Feeder that had dominated the sinking of Haswell, Hetton, Wearmouth and Murton collieries in the first half of the nineteenth century had deterred further attempts to go beneath the limestone. With this new method, Dawdon, Easington, Horden and Blackhall collieries were sunk. These massive coal-producing machines employed thousands of hewers working the high seams under the North Sea. While these giants of modern mining were constructed in the east, the high quality of the west of Durham coking coal kept miners employed in narrow seams in primitive conditions that would change little until they closed.

In 1908 an Act of Parliament was passed restricting the hours of labour of all underground men to a shift of not longer than eight hours. While the DMA reached agreement with the owners that the hewers' hours would remain unchanged at between six-and-a-half and seven hours, depending on the colliery, the owners of some collieries changed the shift pattern to accommodate the shorter shift for putters and back-bye workers. A wave of strikes affected collieries in 1910. During a riot at Horden colliery the miners burnt down the club that the owners had built. There were similar disturbances at Murton and Anfield Plain.

In 1907 the men in Durham voted 67,986 to 18,983 for the DMA to join the Miners' Federation of Great Britain (MFGB). This welded British miners into the first truly national miners' union.

At the same time as these great changes in organisation, the miners of Durham were also playing their part in the new political developments taking place in the British working class: the spread of socialist ideas and agitation for an independent political party of the working class. This move towards the formation of the Labour Representation Committee in 1900 and then the Labour Party in 1906 was something which had been strongly opposed by Wilson, Cann and other leaders of the union in Durham. Their policies were essentially ones of conciliation with the employers and working politically only through the Liberal Party in parliament.

But the election of Keir Hardie as MP for Mid-Lanark in 1888 marked the beginning of a rapid spread of socialist teaching and organisation. The Independent Labour Party, formed in 1893, sent its national organiser, Tom Taylor, to Durham. The famous Tom Mann of the Social-Democratic Federation, an organisation of Marxists, addressed dozens of well-attended meetings in the mining villages, preaching socialism. This helped to fuel the growing criticism of the DMA leaders, and when Tom Mann was invited as a speaker to the Gala in 1901, he declared from the platform that 'it was no secret that he had never been at the Gala by the wish of the miners' Executive'. He chose the occasion to attack the class-collaboration policies of John Wilson in particular.

Wilson was to continue in office as 'Lib-Lab' MP until 1915, but by then the tide had long since turned in the coalfield. Speaking at the 1914 Gala, Jim Larkin was reported as saying: 'If we are to have an independent Labour Party, for God's sake let it be independent and not connected with the flabby, vindictive Liberal Party'.

Thomas Cann had pronounced in 1906: 'Personally I should be very sorry to see the union captured by the socialists.' But the Council meeting of that same year carried the Lintz Green resolution: 'To support labour candidates independent of any political party'.

Things were now moving rapidly. In 1907 Durham miners voted to join the MFGB. In the following year the MFGB affiliated to the newly-formed Labour Party, and in December the Durham Council amended the DMA's rules to read that political candidates must 'run in

Keir Hardie

conformity with the rules and constitution of the Labour Party'.

John Wilson refused to sign, and George Harvey published an article entitled 'Does Dr John Wilson

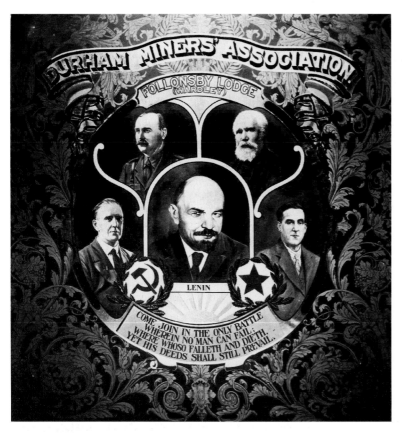

Follonsby Banner - centre, Lenin; outer portraits left to right:
A J Cook; James Conolly; Keir Hardie; George Harvey.

The decision of the DMA to join the MFGB effectively united British miners into one organisation which was a federation of independent trades unions. Strengthened by Durham's decision to join, the MFGB soon faced the test of a great miners' struggle: the minimum wage strike of 1912, the first nationwide strike of miners. The support and solidarity for this great strike was the culmination of determined and continuous agitation for a minimum wage in the preceding years.

In the South Wales coalfield the conflict preceding the strike was at its sharpest, indeed bloodiest, with a series of events that inflamed the mood nationally. In October 1910, the firm of Cambrian Collieries Ltd had tried to enforce a new low piece-rate of 1s 9d a ton. The men demanded 2s 6d on the grounds that the difficult strata qualified them for an 'abnormal place' allowance. The company responded by locking out not only the men in dispute but the whole workforce of 800 at the Ely pit.

The South Wales Miners Federation called out all 1,200 Cambrian Combine miners. These were joined by the miners of the Aberdare valley,

serve the working class?' Harvey was sued for libel by Wilson, who won the case, but the incident made Harvey very popular. Born at Beamish in 1885, he had studied at Ruskin College and was a member of the Socialist Labour Party. In 1913 he became checkweighman at Follonsby (Wardley) colliery.

making the total on strike 30,000.

Miners marched on the nearby Glamorgan Colliery when they heard reports that blacklegs were being imported. In Tonypandy windows were smashed, and the police dispersed the miners indiscriminately by brutal use of their truncheons. The Chief Constable of Glamorgan contacted Winston Churchill, the Home Secretary, soon to become the miners' arch-enemy. In a matter of hours Churchill ordered five hundred Metropolitan police to reinforce Glamorgan's six hundred, and appointed General Macready to command all police and troops in the area.

In parliament Keir Hardie exposed incidents of gross police violence in Tonypandy and in Aberaman in his own constituency, Merthyr Tydfil. Tonypandy became a byword for the use of state repression and violence against the miners, to be repeated time and again.

It was a year before the Cambrian Combine strikers returned to work, on terms very little different from those they could have had at the time of the lockout. The suffering in the coalfield had a terrific impact nationally. Four months after the strike had begun, the February 1911 special conference of the MFGB called for the dispute to be settled by arbitration. The Tonypandy delegate

Tom Smith told the Conference:

> If you think that arbitration offered by this Federation is going to be a means of effecting a settlement we offer no objection. If the owners refuse arbitration, then I take it the Federation is going to take up the whole question of the strike, and see it through. In South Wales men are starving, women are starving, children are starving. I can tell you that women are bringing children into the world without a rag to cover them when they are born. I know of children who have been born in houses where there has been nothing, not a single bit of clothing to put on them. If ever there was intense suffering, that suffering is in South Wales. If ever there was intense heroism manifested, it has been by the women and children in this struggle. I take it if arbitration is offered by this great Federation and is refused, then you are not going to allow us to starve any longer.

The owners refused arbitration, but said they would discuss. After two weeks' discussion, terms of settlement were drawn up by the owners' representatives together with miners' leaders and MPs Edwards, Ashton, Abraham and Richards. The MFGB executive agreed to these terms, but they were angrily rejected by South Wales. The following months saw bitter exchanges between the national leaders. Refusing solidarity action and insisting on the 'settlement', Ashton and his associates condemned what they called 'anarchy' and constantly referred to 'those who want not a settlement but only to continue the strike', and Derbyshire MP Harvey referred in Conference to 'howling mobs' in South Wales. These leaders and their policies were roundly condemned by the South Wales men who, by August, were being forced to recognise that they had been left isolated. When the final return came in October, some 3,000 men did not get their jobs back.

As historian Robin Page Arnot justly concluded:

> The Cambrian Combine men, in the course of their struggle, had raised the question of abnormal places to be a national mining issue and in the later stages had carried this still farther to the issue of a National Minimum Wage. To this they had converted the whole of the South Wales coalfield and were presently to convert the whole of the miners of the United Kingdom. They had lost their local dispute; they had won the desired national movement to settle the wider question. The strike with all its bitter hardship and suffering had not been in vain.

There had been a continuous build-up of grievances, coalowners' attacks, disputes and conflicts in the years immediately leading up to the great 1912 minimum wage strike. The Coal Mines Act of 1911, secured after 20 years of agitation by the MFGB, was a real step forward in establishing safety standards for miners but its inadequate implementation by recalcitrant and ruthless coal owners was a spur to conflict everywhere. Only two years after the Act, the worst disaster in mining history occurred at the Senghenydd pit (Glamorgan): four hundred and thirty-nine men perished in a colliery where the danger of gas explosion had been known for certain since 1910. When derisory fines of £5 and £10 were handed to the pit manager, the local paper headlined its report: 'MINERS' LIVES AT 1s 1d EACH.'

Like other districts, Durham followed the MFGB annual conference resolution for a minimum wage by attempting to get satisfaction from local negotiations, the employers always insisting that national negotiations were out of the question. Special MFGB Conferences attempted to bring the coal owners to the table at national level, but when this was finally achieved on 29 September 1911, the employers remained obstinate. Now a national dispute was becoming inevitable. Durham, Lancashire and Cheshire, Somerset and Yorkshire put resolutions to conference on the necessity of a minimum wage, and there was unanimous agreement. The final resolution read:

> That the Federation take immediate steps to secure an individual District Minimum Wage for all men and boys working in mines in the area of the Federation without any reference to the working places being abnormal. In the event of the employers refusing to agree to this then the amended 21st rule of the Federation

Miners Federation of Great Britain Executive Committee, October 1913.
Back row: J McGurk; W Straker; S Roebuck; J G Hancock; V Hartshorn; J Robson; H Murnin; G Barker; A Sharp;
J Robertson. Front row: S H Whitehouse; A Stanley; T Ashton; R Smillie; W E Harvey; J Wilson; W Brace.

[sanctioning national action in support of men in any district - ed.] be put into operation to demand the same. That a Conference be called on November 14th for the purpose of taking action under rule 21.

Especially in Durham, the owners stubbornly insisted that the very principle of a minimum wage was unacceptable. According to them, it would mean men would be 'shirking', instead of performing the tasks they were paid for. John Cairns of Northumberland, moving a resolution for a ballot for strike action, told the November special conference that he had been asked by one coalowner, 'one of our magnates, a big landlord', the reason for the 'unrest' among the miners, and that he had replied:

> Our men have been under the thumbs of the schoolmasters from at least 1870 until now and our men are more refined than they were forty years ago; they desire better homes, better food, better clothing, better conditions.

However, influenced by Bob Smillie and other

speakers, including Durham's Alderman House, the November Conference voted 376 to 238 to postpone a decision until 'further efforts be made to bring about a satisfactory settlement'. But when they met again on 20 December the die was cast, the owners having replied that 'no useful purpose would be served' by negotiations. Warned now by Smillie that 'we are face to face with the most serious crisis that the miners of this country or any other country have ever met with', the December conference resolved to ballot the members on 10, 11 and 12 January 1912. John Wilson MP pointed out that Durham had a rule necessitating a two-thirds majority for action, and so the national conference finally resolved:

That in case the ballot results in a two-thirds majority in favour of a national stoppage, notice be given in every district, so as to terminate at the end of February 1912.

> In the event, the ballot showed 445,801 for strike action, with 115,921 against, a four-to-one majority. In Durham 57,490 voted for, with 28,504 against.

A last-ditch meeting with the employers on 7 February showed complete deadlock, the owners seemingly ready to face what would obviously be the biggest miners' strike in history. This was a fact recognised by miners internationally. When the MFGB leaders called together the Miners'

International Committee and met the leaders of miners in France, Belgium, Germany and Austria, they agreed that in the event of a strike no coal would come from the Continent to Britain, something that could be assured by working one day a week less. They carried a further resolution:

> That if the miners in any of the Continental Nations at the present time or in the future agree to demand an individual minimum wage and declare a strike to secure it, or enter upon a strike to remedy any other grievances, the miners of Great Britain agree to recommend that the output of Great Britain be curtailed as far as possible.

Here was a mark of the miners' tradition of international solidarity that has always been particularly strong amongst the miners of Durham.

Despite the owners' intransigence on 7 February the MFGB , 'since they had no desire for a serious rupture in the coal trade of the country', made unprecedented efforts to get a settlement, calling no less than four special conferences in February and March.

The magnitude of the impending battle was unmistakably shown by the government's decision to intervene. The 1893 government had allowed the great lockout to go on for four months before acting. Now, in the third week of February 1912, before the strike began, Prime Minister

Asquith wrote to the MFGB's Thomas Ashton: 'Sir, His Majesty's government have watched with close attention and growing anxiety the development of the present crisis in the coal trade', and offered to mediate 'to avert the disaster of a national stoppage'.

Seaham strike committee 20 April 1912 Back row: G Lee, R Rutherford, A Rochester, R Tempest, J Morris
Third row: J Burns, M Scally, P Henderson, P Sullivan, W Frost, J English, G McGann
Second row: Mercer, J Hepple, J Huges. J Crane, T Braddock, R Collings (Delegate) J Hoy(Secretary), J Alexander
(President), J Self (Treasurer), G Heckle, M Duffy Front row: T Price, W Savage, J Stephenson, F Tate, E. Temple

One reason for the government's anxiety was undoubtedly the way it had been shaken, indeed frightened, by the national railway strike in August 1911 and the seamen's strike in June of that year, in which the ports of London and Liverpool had been stopped. Webb's *History of Trade Unionism* states:

> The War Office, at the request of Mr. Winston Churchill, who was then at the Home Office, accumulated troops in London, and actually threatened to put 25,000 soldiers to break the strike by doing the dockers' work, a step that would undoubtedly have led to bloody conflict in the streets.

Asquith called the whole MFGB Conference (170 men!) to the Foreign Office on 27 February. He bent over backwards to persuade them to call off the strike, even verbally conceding in principle that a minimum wage was justified. The government's eventual proposal, however, entailed compulsory state arbitration when district agreements could not be reached, and miners had always rejected such arbitration. Nor did the employers accept the government's proposal; the Prime Minister told the House of Commons that they were now faced with 'not a breakdown but a deadlock'.

On 1 March 1912, with the inevitability of night following day, 800,000 miners came out. It was the first day of the biggest strike in British history, in which a total of one million men were soon out. The coalfields were solid as a rock, despite the meagre strike pay and great privation in every coalfield. The coal owners folded their arms and waited, having big stocks of coal at the time and now being able to command high prices. But, from the second week in March, the situation was changing and stocks were depleted.

Factories went on short-time and many closed. Train services everywhere were cut, and railwaymen, transport workers and many others were put out of work. Coal was then of course the sole means of domestic and institutional heating, and the shortages soon led to severe problems.

Many public figures had sought to stop the strike, such was the universal concern at the prospect of its effects. The government sought another meeting with the miners' leaders after one week of the strike, but only to ask if they had modified their demand, to which they replied 'No'. Persisting, the government called the two sides together for a discussion on 12, 13 and 14 March. The miners' leaders reported back continuously to their special conference. The government's formula included compulsory negotiation which was rejected by the miners' spokesmen, a decision unanimously endorsed by the conference delegates. The employers rejected all proposed terms for a settlement. It was still deadlock.

Enoch Edwards now reported to the Conference:

> The government have abandoned all hope of ever coming to an agreement with the employers. Mr. Asquith has told us that they shall bring in a Bill to compel the owners to pay a minimum wage.

The strike had remained completely solid, in Durham as everywhere else, and the miners' leaders were hoping for a real advance through the promised Bill, which was introduced to Parliament on 19 March. Although conceding the principle of a minimum wage, the government deliberately included no figures, leaving the amount to be decided by district agreements. Perhaps they hoped in this way to divide the miners. On the same day the arrest of Tom Mann

Cornsay colliery, Chapel flat, circa 1910

was ordered which inflamed the situation.

It was not long before signs of division began to appear. On the introduction of the Bill, there was unanimity on the following resolution:

> No Act of Parliament which does not provide for the inclusion of a minimum wage of not less than 5s per day for all adult workers other than pieceworkers, and 2s a day for boys at 14, will be acceptable to the workmen. (March 20)

However, the leadership put a resolution that the Bill 'ought to contain the schedule rates for hewers in each separate district'.

Many delegates considered that this 'ought' instead of 'must' showed a weakening of the leaders under the pressure of the Prime Minister and Lloyd George, and an amendment stating the actual figures for hewers must be contained in the Bill was passed, against the leadership, by 321 votes to 269.

As the Bill made its way through its Second Reading and Report Stage in the next three days, the miners' leaders thought they had been given strong hints by the government that the figures they wished included were to be in the final version, but this proved not to be so, and the leaders stated that they had been 'led up the garden path'. The Bill had its final reading on 27 March, to become law on 29 March, and MFGB

Conference felt obliged to declare its mandate exhausted, and decided to ballot the members on whether to continue or to end the strike.

Throughout the coalfields there was a strong feeling that the miners had been cheated. The Liberal government had pretended to be neutral, even to favour the miners' case, but in fact had sided with the owners, and the Bill gave no more than had already been conceded in principle before the strike by the majority of owners in the English coalfields. No one knew what the minimum rates of pay were to be.

The ballot paper contained no recommendation from the leadership. The result showed 244,011 to continue against 201,013 to go back. The number voting to go back was swollen by the vote in South Wales, previously perhaps the most militant area. No doubt the great hardship caused by the ravages of the recent Cambrian Combine struggle had sapped the resolve of the miners. In Durham the vote to continue was 48,828 against 24,511 to go back.

The largest area, South Wales, had voted to return, together with the Midlands, and the leaders believed that there was a danger of disunity if the strike were to continue, with employers in some districts conceding and others not. Furthermore, though nothing had been gained for miners in the

English coalfields, Scotland and South Wales now did have the principle of minimum wage recognised. The executive resolved on a return to work, using the two-thirds stipulation which had been made when the strike was called. Although in the English coalfields there was in fact a two-thirds majority to continue, the executive passed the following resolution on 4 April:

> Seeing that there is no provision in the rules or regulations of the Federation to guide this Committee as to the majority required to continue the strike, except the resolution passed at the Conference held 21 December 1911, that a two-thirds majority be required to declare a national strike, we agree that the same majority be required to continue the strike; and seeing that a two-thirds majority is not in favour of continuance of the strike, and acting upon that vote, we advise the resumption of work.

Put to the Special Conference of 6 April, this was accepted on a card vote by 449,500 against 125,000, only Yorkshire and Lancashire being opposed. By the end of April all miners were back at work.

Six weeks of national strike on behalf of a minority of pitmen, on a basic principle, had looked certain of victory, only for the miners to be tricked by the government. They

Miners at Lilly drift Ryton, 1910

returned to work bitterly disappointed, even if it can be said, in hindsight, that this national action showed that the Miners' Federation now constituted beyond doubt a powerful and united fighting force, and that their experience at the hands of the Liberal government consolidated the conviction that the working class must have its own, independent political party.

Eldon colliery, Bishop Auckland 1910

Robert Smillie

Chapter 5

In the aftermath of the 1912 minimum wage strike, the hard and painstaking work of confronting the owners and negotiating rates of pay had to proceed. At the same time, the Miners' Federation turned to other great issues.

In July 1912, Smillie was the driving force behind the move to press for nationalisation of the mines. As long ago as the fifth MFGB conference in 1894, delegates had passed a resolution by 158 votes to 50: 'That in the opinion of this conference, the best interests of the nation will be served by the nationalisation of the mines of the country,' and the issue had been raised in similarly general terms at successive conferences. The demand came to be seen as a more realistic prospect and gathered momentum as the Labour Party began to win parliamentary seats. But it was not until 1912, when Smillie became acting vice-president, that the issue was concretised. In July the MFGB executive appointed a subcommittee to draft a Bill for introduction into parliament. This was done, and the annual conference in October 1912 resolved unanimously: 'That the principles contained in the Mines Nationalisation Bill as drafted by the Committee be and are hereby approved.' The executive was instructed by conference 'to carry on the agitation'.

When the draft Bill was submitted to the Labour Party, it was returned with a list of amendments, one of which proposed to pay compensation to the owners. This the MFGB firmly rejected. When introduced to the Commons, the Bill did not even get discussed, and it was 1918 before there were any further developments.

In 1911 the executive had been instructed by conference to 'take the necessary steps' to ensure a five-day working week and in 1912 it decided to ballot the membership on a campaign. But when the result showed a majority of 253,541 for to

209,826 against, it was considered unwise to go forward to a fight. The old issue of a two-thirds majority had raised its head again, and the special conference of 27 March 1913 decided to lay down an unambiguous ruling:

> That before a national strike is entered upon as the result of any finding of a conference, a ballot vote of the members shall be taken, and a strike shall not be declared unless two-thirds of those voting vote in favour of such a strike. If a ballot vote be taken during the time a strike is in progress a vote of two-thirds of those taking part in the ballot shall be necessary to continue the strike.

The next matter of great concern was the infamous 1909 'Osborne Judgment', which denied trade unions the right to take part in politics. In 1910 the miners' unions in several MFGB districts had injunctions taken against them for raising a political levy from the members to support the sending of approved candidates to parliament, a long-standing practice in miners' unions. Now that right was in danger of being lost completely. Together with the Labour Party, the MFGB attempted to get the law changed, but, as Page Arnot remarks:

> The Liberal Party had too many coalowners and shipowners among its prominent supporters to be in favour of promoting legislation which would restore the situation of the law as it was generally understood to be before the Osborne Judgment was delivered.

Labour Party election rally Durham

However, the Liberal government of the day needed the few Labour votes in the Commons to stay in office and for this reason they had attempted a compromise in the form of a Bill early in 1911. A Labour Party special conference rejected this, and Asquith promised an improved Bill in 1912. Meanwhile, at the instigation of employers, the courts placed new restrictions on the payment of affiliation fees to the Labour Party by the MFGB. However, when the Trade Union Act of 1913 was passed, there was provision for trade unions to spend money on purposes proper to 'the objects of trade unions' and defined in their constitutions. For political purposes, defined by the Act, money could be spent only after a secret ballot of the members approved and there was specific provision for individual members to 'contract out' of the political levy. Although the MFGB executive had put a resolution to the special conference which said 'no measure or Bill can be accepted as satisfactory that does not completely reverse the Osborne decision', the same resolution concluded that the present Bill must be accepted 'for the time being, subject to any further improvements or amendments that can be obtained during the further passage of the Bill'.

Once the Act was in force, the MFGB constituted a single body for political purposes under the Act, and proceeded to write into its rules the political purposes for which it would spend money, including support of parliamentary candidates. When this went to members' ballot it was supported by 261,643 votes for, 194,800 against.

The ambition of reversing the Osborne Judgment remained unfulfilled.

In 1913 a decision was taken to form the Triple Alliance of the MFGB, the National Union of Railwaymen and the National Transport Workers' Federation, with the stated object of supporting each other's demands.

In 1912 the pressure by many trade unionists and Labour Party members for a working-class newspaper as an alternative to the capitalist press came to a head. This resulted in the production of the *Daily Citizen* and George Lansbury's more left-wing *Daily Herald*, which became very popular. The *Citizen* soon folded.

There were also political developments in the field of working-class education. Ruskin College, Oxford, founded in 1899, had been attended by miners and other workers from many areas, who afterwards often became influential in their unions. But when in 1908 the governors of Ruskin objected to the Marxist views of the then principal, Dennis Nird, the majority of the students, among them George Harvey, took strike action.

They withdrew from Ruskin and, with the support of the South Wales Miners' Federation and the National Union of Railwaymen, set up the Central Labour College, with the slogan of 'independent working-class education'. Durham was one of the areas in which this idea took hold, and there were regular classes in many villages. In 1918 the National Council of Labour Colleges (NCLC) was founded.

It is appropriate, here, to glance at the conditions of home life in the coalfields. This is perhaps best done through an example taken from County

Durham and reproduced from Page Arnot's history of the miners:

Shortly before the father, working in Northumberland, sought work across the Tyne in county Durham, the eldest son (of nine sons and two daughters) had to leave school and go to work in the pit when he was only 12 years of age. At the age of 13 the next son began work at the colliery and so with the third son. Each successive son at work in the pits meant more toil for the mother at home.

The mother of this family gave the following account of her daily life, confirmed by one of her sons:

The day began at 3a.m. when the eldest son, a hewer, made his breakfast, took his 'bait' put up the night before and went on shift at 4a.m. Mother, if awake, would try and snatch an hour's sleep before preparing a younger son, a datal worker, whose shift started at 6a.m. He would no sooner be off than Father would be coming in for breakfast-and-bath, his shift ending at 6a.m. He had started his shift at 10p.m. the previous night. The repair shift worked a full eight-hour shift plus winding while the hewers worked six-and-a-half to seven hours per shift. In spite of the longer hours the repair workers had a smaller basic wage than the hewers.

By the time Father had had his breakfast and bathed in a tin in front of the fire it would be

Miner's wife at work

time for three children to get up and prepare for school. Even with this task performed, Mother had no time to rest. She now had to prepare a dinner for the eldest, returning between 11 and 11.30a.m. He would not have finished washing in front of the fire before the children returned from school for their midday meal. In all probability Father would get up and have something with the children at midday, go to the local for a pint, return at tea time and go to bed for a couple of hours.

With the children off to school for the afternoon Mother had to prepare for three more sons going on shift at 2p.m. By the time she had got them off she had to prepare a meal and bathing water for the son who went on shift at 6a.m. and would be returning to the house just after 2p.m. By the time he was off the kitchen floor it was nearly time for the school children returning. On top of this continual round all the washing 'laundry' was done at home, as well as baking. There was no bought bread in northern mining villages in those days. The bread was all baked at home. This took sacks and sacks of flour.

Then she had to prepare for Father going on shift at 10p.m.

The next preparation was the biggest of the day. After 10p.m. the three sons who had gone on shift at 2p.m. would be home. Not only had Mother to prepare their meals on the kitchen fire, but she had also to boil the water for their bath in pan and kettle. Altogether it would take anything up to two hours before they were all bathed, which they took successively in a tin on the hearth in front of the fire. It was always after midnight before they were all off to bed. This was the end of a normal day and the alarm clock would ring again at 3a.m. for another day.

Such was the lot of the wives of the more than one hundred thousand miners of County Durham for generations.

War was declared in 1914 and within seven months 191,000 men had enlisted; two months later the number had risen to 220,000, and by August 1915 to over a quarter of a million. That the cream of the Durham's youth enlisted was no doubt a reflection of the dreadful conditions of life and work in the coalfield. For those left at home there was the agonising wait for letters and the misery when the almost inevitable black-bordered telegram dropped through the letter box.

This war put the newly formed Labour Party to its first great test. The Labour Party was affiliated to the Socialist International, as were the German Social Democrats. At the 1912 Basel Congress the Socialist International had passed the following resolution (resembling several resolutions of earlier years), to which the Labour Party and its affiliate, the MFGB, were committed:

> If war threatens to break out it is the duty of the working class in the countries concerned and of their parliamentary representatives, with the help of the International Socialist Bureau as means of coordinating their action, to use every effort to prevent war by all the means which seem to them most appropriate, having regard to the sharpness of the class war and to the general political situation.

Should war none the less break out, their duty is to intervene to bring it promptly to an end, and with all their energies to use the political and economic crisis created by the war to rouse the populace from its slumbers and to hasten the fall of capitalist domination.

On 29 August 1914, twenty-five days after the declaration of war, the British Labour Party decided:

That, in view of the serious situation created by the European war, the Executive Committee of the Labour Party agrees with the policy of the parliamentary party, in joining the campaign to strengthen the British Army, and agrees to place

Redhaugh colliery Gateshead 1920

the Central Office organisation at the disposal of the campaign, and further recommends the affiliated bodies to give all possible local support.

Similarly, in Germany the Social-Democratic Party voted to support the provision of credits for the conduct of Germany's war effort.

The Labour Party then took Cabinet posts in the coalition government.

Among the many in the working-class movement who opposed this change in policy was Will Lawther of Chopwell, member of the DMA executive, later to become President of the MFGB. But their opposition was to no avail and those who opposed the war were, in the main, isolated.

During the war, the conflict between workers, particularly miners, and their employers did not cease. In the first months the coalowners in some districts withdrew their demands for reductions, but in Durham the employers imposed wage-cuts on 200,000 miners. By the end of 1914 when the mass enlistment of miners led to serious shortage of coal the alarm was sounded, and the employers took the opportunity to campaign for the suspension of the Eight Hours Act, as well as seeking the right to employ women on the pit-top and boys under the permitted age underground.

The Commission appointed to look into the crisis refused them these benefits, but called on miners to make greater efforts.

Miners' wages had steadily declined in value over the last twenty years, but the inflation, especially in food prices, which had risen by 20 per cent, inevitably brought matters to a head. In March 1915 the miners demanded a 20-per-cent increase on earnings. The employers at first refused national negotiations, and when the government intervened and offered 10 per cent, the MFGB refused, referring the 20 per cent demand to the Prime Minister for settlement by arbitration. Asquith declared that an immediate increase was justified, but that the actual amount should be left to local negotiations.

The results were very uneven. Durham and Northumberland miners fared worst of all, employers conceding only 15 per cent on the standard rate, which amounted to less than half of the 20 per cent on earnings which had been demanded. By contrast, the Federated Districts got over 15 per cent on earnings. No one got 20 per cent, and Asquith, in line with the express interests of the employers, ruled out a national wage agreement, that long-standing aspiration of the MFGB.

Notice was given by the MFGB to terminate the

Miners dividing up their pay

existing Conciliation Board agreements (containing standards dating from 1877, 1879 and 1888) by 1 April 1915. At the same time a demand was posted for a minimum wage of at least 5s per day for all surface workers. Furthermore it was resolved that all District agreements must be confirmed by the MFGB. These demands were in large part met, except in South Wales, which sparked the biggest industrial conflict of the war years.

When the South Wales miners gave notice to end the existing agreement and made the same demands, the owners prevaricated and the government intervened making more unacceptable proposals and creating yet more frustrating postponements. A delegate conference in Wales resolved on 12 July 1915 by an almost two-to-one majority:

> We do not accept anything less than our original proposals, and . . . we stop the collieries on Thursday next until these terms are conceded.

Immediately the government implemented its wartime power to ban strikes, making the miners even more determined. They came out to a man. Faced with the ridiculous prospect of fining 200,000 men, and in fear of the consequences, the government intervened after five days and negotiated a settlement favourable to the men.

This agreement did not prevent running wage disputes in South Wales, and in November 1916 the government declared the coalfield under state control under the Defence of the Realm Act. In December it was announced that state control was to be extended to the whole industry by February 1917.

State control was supposed to control output and distribution, but its effectiveness was slight because of the way in which the coalowners were able to ensure that, in all matters, the first charge on the industry was their profits.

The precipitous decline in living standards caused

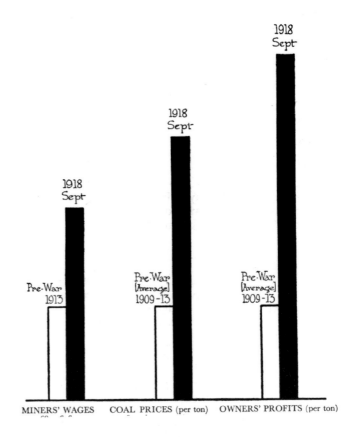

by the increasing rate of inflation fuelled more wage struggles at national level. The ceaseless blood-letting on the killing fields of northern France and Belgium decimated a generation of young men in scores of pit villages and war-weariness set in.

The vicious shooting of James Connolly after the suppression of the Easter Rising for Irish independence in 1916 produced widespread revulsion in the working class. Some miners, one of whom was Arthur Horner, a future general Secretary of the NUM, crossed into Ireland to help the Sinn Feiners.

The February and October 1917 revolutions in Russia inspired a radicalisation in Britain, as in the rest of the world. The growing feelings of sickness at the war intensified when the victorious Bolsheviks published the secret treaties of the Allies.

It was in this new political situation that the national wages battle was renewed. The November 1918 Armistice ended the war; but heralded a new stage in the war between classes, with the miners in the front line.

Sherburn House colliery 1920

Fishburn colliery 1920

Pit boys at Emma colliery 1926

Chapter 6

The First World War was at an end. After the flags and bunting had been put away, an explosive combination of raised expectations and broken promises ignited in 1919. On 27 January the shipyard and engineering workers of the Clyde struck work for a 40-hour week. The government replied by moving troops and tanks into Glasgow and arresting the strike leaders.

Two weeks earlier the Miners' Federation of Great Britain had resolved to demand a 30-per-cent increase in wages, a six-hour working day, and the nationalisation of the mines, giving control of the industry to the miners. To achieve these demands, 615,000 miners voted to strike, with 105,000 against. The government of Lloyd George was well advised to fear a Miners' strike. Coal stocks were low and the miners had combined with the rail and transport Unions to form what became known as the Triple Alliance. Both the other arms of this alliance had their own demands on the table, putting the government under further pressure. Under these conditions the government reached a compromise, and set up the Sankey Commission to make recommendations on the question of wages, hours and the control of the industry.

Expecting a favourable outcome, the MFGB withdrew the strike notices pending the Commission's interim report. The interim report awarded a 2s-per-shift increase in pay, a reduction in the working day from eight to seven hours and, more important in the view of many miners, a commitment to the nationalisation of the industry, even if in somewhat vague terms. These recommendations were accepted by the MFGB but it soon became all too clear that the government had made concessions in order to gain time. Almost immediately the government coal controller announced that no more than 10-per-cent increases in piece-rate prices were to be sanctioned. It took a bitter strike in South Yorkshire, in the course of which soldiers and naval ratings were used to keep order, to force a withdrawal of this order.

In October 1920 the miners again issued strike notices demanding a further increase in wages. It was now that the Triple Alliance was put to its first test. The Miners' strike notice had expired on 16 October, but it was not until 21 October that a special

Army mobilisation 1926

delegate conference of railwaymen agreed to strike in their support on the 24th. An interim agreement due to expire on 31 March 1921 was put forward by Lloyd George. This was rejected by a Miners' ballot, but while there was a clear majority of 8,000, it failed to reach the two-thirds majority required to continue the strike.

Leaders 1926

Black Friday

Once again the owners and the government had bought time. By February 1921 they felt strong enough to announce that the limited government control of the coal industry initiated during the First World War was to end. The owners, now back at the helm, announced wage cuts and an end to all national agreements. When the miners refused to accept these cuts they were locked out.

On 8 April the Triple Alliance declared a strike of railwaymen and transport workers in solidarity with the miners. The government responded by declaring a State of Emergency. Machine-gun posts were set up at pit-heads and troops were drafted into all working-class areas.

Once again the Alliance wavered. First 12 April was given as the date for the sympathy strike to begin; later this was changed to 15 April. CT Cramp and JH Thomas of the rail union sought to open negotiations between the government and the miners' leaders. On 15 April Thomas, having failed to bring the government and the miners' leaders together, called off their sympathy action. This day came to be known as Black Friday, remembered by miners as a day of treachery.

Arthur Cook addressing meeting 1926

MFGB leaders Smith, Hodges and Robson met the Prime Minister at Chequers on the weekend of 27 June to get the government to agree to give the subsidy if there was a return to work. This action of the MFGB leaders brought strong criticism from the Durham area and miners at Leadgate called for the resignation of the entire committee.

After a delegate conference recommended a return to work on the basis of area bargaining the lock-out ended at the end of June. Almost immediately Durham was plunged into a trade depression that left one-fifth of the miners out of work and over one hundred collieries standing idle.

Red Friday

In the years following 1921 the whole of the British working class was ground down into poverty. The defeat of the miners had opened the gate to a general attack on wages and conditions. By 1925 the coalowners were again seeking further reductions. On 30 June they announced

Of all areas, Durham was among the most adamant that the struggle against area bargaining must continue. The wages formula proposed by the owners tied wages to the selling price of coal. Durham, being an exporting coalfield, was subject to large variations in the selling price of its coal and thus would be a major loser if the owners' system was adopted. In this they were supported by the majority of miners in the country, who rejected the coalowners' proposals by a majority of two to one in June 1921. The government then withdrew its offer of a temporary subsidy of £10m to alleviate the worst effects of the reductions. Despite the miners' ballot rejecting this formula, the end to all national agreements, the abolition of the minimum wage and a return to local bargaining. When the Miners' Federation rejected the owners' demands, they were supported by the General Council of the TUC, who threatened supportive action if the miners were locked out.

Prime Minister Baldwin and his lieutenant, Winston Churchill, were at this point unprepared for conflict. Again they played for time and introduced a nine-month subsidy to the coal owners to maintain wages while a Royal Commission under the chairmanship of Lord Samuel sat to compile a report on the industry. The employers withdrew their lock-out notices on what became known as Red Friday.

With little time to lose the government began

Lodge officials of Chopwell (Little Moscow) Lodge, Left to right: Jack Lawther, Will Lawther, Steve Lawther, Jack Gilland, Ned Wilson, Jim Stephenson, Edd Lawther.

frantically to prepare for the coming conflict. Churchill was put in charge and set about constructing his strike-breaking machine, the 'Organisation for the Maintenance of Supplies'.

In contrast, the TUC, with the now-hated Thomas on its General Council, refused to do anything until the Samuel Commission gave its report.

The Labour Party declared: 'We transcend the conflict of classes; we call for the co-operation of all classes.'

While the Miners' Federation under the leadership of AJ Cook tried to put together a new industrial alliance they were thwarted, mainly due to the sabotage of Thomas. On 10 March the Samuel Commission gave its report, coming down heavily against any continuation of the subsidy to the coal industry. Inherent in the report was the assumption that an adjustment in wages and hours of work was inevitable, and that there should be variation on a local basis. Even Baldwin, the Tory Prime Minister, intervened on 22 April to try to get the owners to agree to a national wages system, but failed. The employers responded with a series of wage reductions based on an eight-hour day.

The question of hours affected Durham acutely. Durham miners had developed working practices that had resulted in hewers, the majority of the men employed, working only six hours in some cases at the coal face. As long ago as 1890 an agreement with the Durham coalowners provided for no hewer to work more than seven hours, bank to bank. In many cases, local agreements provided shorter hours.

A further factor complicated the Durham situation: several collieries were already locked out. On 22 June 1925 the collieries owned by the Consett Iron Company, Chopwell, Langley Park, Westwood, Medomsley, and Derwent, were locked out when they refused to agree to a new wages structure. St Hilda's Colliery in South Shields was also in dispute. On 3 May 1926, failing to reach an agreement with the government, the General Council of the TUC invited its constituent unions to call their members out on strike. For the men at these pits hopes must have risen that their year-long ordeal was over. It was not to be.

In Durham the response was swift. By 3 May, two hundred pits were idle. They were soon supported by shipyard, engineering and power workers. The whole region was at a standstill. Whereas the government had made extensive preparations for the dispute, the TUC had made none whatsoever, and it fell to the local leadership at pit and workshop level to organise the activity of the strikers. A call came from the militant village of Chopwell to organise local Councils of Action to take charge of the

Marsden soup kitchen 1926

distribution of food, picketing, and the dissemination of propaganda. The slowness of the Miners' Agents based at Durham to respond to this call to action caused an immediate rift between the leaders and the rank and file that lasted for the duration of the strike.

For the government, the General Strike was nothing less than an act of revolution, and full support was conferred on the armed forces to do what was required to defend 'Civil Power'. If the government was frightened by the enthusiasm

with which the rank and file had responded to the General Strike call, the TUC leaders were petrified. On the weekend of 7-10 May, behind the backs of the miners' leaders, they met with Samuel to negotiate an end to the strike based on his report, accepting a reduction in pay and an increase in hours.

When the miners were told of the proposals, the leaders of the MFGB rejected them, but since the dispute was in the hands of the General Council, the miners' leaders had no power of veto. Failing to persuade the miners to accept the Samuel proposals, the TUC General Council sent a deputation under the leadership of A Pugh to meet the Prime Minister at Downing Street and inform him that they were calling off the General Strike unconditionally.

Never was there a more bitter moment in the history of the British miners and the working-class movement.

Despite the demoralising effect this great betrayal must have had on the miners and their families in Durham, and despite the determination of the coalowners to introduce an eight-hour day for all classes of miners, the resolve of the men to defend their six-to-six-and-three-quarter hours underground galvanised the county into a solid and defiant body. So determined were Durham miners to resist, whatever the hardship, that on more than one occasion there was open conflict with their own Durham Agents, who favoured a compromise.

The summer of 1926 was long and hot and full of hardship. By August substantial numbers of men had returned to work in the Midlands coalfields, which traditionally served the home market and did not have the same economic pressures on their prices as the exporting coalfields of Durham, South Wales and Yorkshire. In Durham, by the end of November, with the hardships of winter already upon them, only 3,000 out of 140,000 miners had returned to work. In the Midlands Federation, mainly due to the insidious activity of the Nottingham Miners' Agent, Spencer, 58,000 of the 97,000 miners had returned to work.

Sensing victory as more men returned in the other coalfields, the employers became more intransigent, more determined to fight to a finish. After one last attempt to get the government to open negotiations at national level, the MFGB recommended each area to negotiate its own return to work.

In Durham the DMA met the owners' association on the 23, 25 and 27 November to negotiate a return to work. The result of these negotiations was a general reduction in wages of about 10 per cent and an increase in hours of all underground workmen to eight hours. There was, however, one important concession given to the hewers: they would be allowed to work seven-and-a-half hours, bank to bank, and their basic rates would be increased to 4s 8d from 4s 2d, in direct proportion to the increase in hours that they would now be working.

In a coalfield ballot held on 29 November these proposals were rejected by a margin of 8,634 votes. Although 63 per cent of the miners voted, the majority had failed to reach the two-thirds required to continue the struggle. The Federation Board therefore instructed the membership to return to work.

Durham had held out for seven months, a month longer than the other coalfields. For the miners of Chopwell their struggle had lasted 18 months. Despite the pledge of the coalowners that there would be no victimisation, hundreds of men were never to work again in the coalfield. Many left with their families, willing to take the chance of a better life in the new mines of Kent, where less would be known of their union activity. For those who stayed, the ordeal was about to begin. They returned to work for less money and longer hours, but this was far from the end of the matter. It was not long before further reductions were demanded and, despite sporadic action, by the end of 1929 miners were working for less than in 1926.

Wearmouth Soup Kitchen 1926

Above: Miners at Pauper Flat Cornsay colliery

Gordon Richardson miner at Railey Drift 1930

Left to right: Sid Raine, Bill Raine, Gordon Richardson Jnr. Tommy Hutchinson at Marshall Green drift, Witton-le-Wear 1940

Unemployed demonstration 1930s, Felling   *Photo: Ancrum collection*

Chapter 7

As soon as the miners were back at work after the collapse of the 1926 strike, Prime Minister Baldwin and his Tory government lost no time in pressing home their advantage. Despite Baldwin's fine talk about an industrial truce, the government passed the notorious Trade Disputes and Trade Union Act which declared illegal any strike not concerned directly with the issues in a trade dispute of a particular group of workers. A strike designed to coerce government was declared illegal and the right to picket was curtailed. The political levy could be paid only by those who specifically 'contracted in'; and no civil servant was allowed to join any union connected with the TUC.

As the general election of 1929 drew near, trade unionists came to place their hopes in the election of a Labour government. However, despite the employers' offensive and the conciliatory attitude of most trade union leaders, miners in more than one instance demonstrated that they were still able to fight.

The coal owners, like the government, sought every possible advantage from the weakened position of the miners, and it was inevitable that Lord Londonderry and his agents should turn their particular attention to Dawdon colliery. Dawdon Lodge had been successful in fighting for agreements to protect their wages from the impact of unfavourable geological conditions before the 1926 dispute. The agreement which Londonderry was especially anxious to get rid of was the so-called 'hitch agreement', which protected earnings whenever the seam being worked moved vertically more than six inches. On 8 January 1929, Londonderry's agent Malcolm Dillon wrote to Frederick Wilson, the Dawdon manager:

> The time has come when it is imperative that the Dawdon costs should be reduced and brought nearer to the county average and practice. This particularly applies to the cost in connection with the hitches which have been very onerous to the colliery for a long period. I shall be very glad if you will take this matter up with the men with a view to obtaining a reduction in costs and putting Dawdon colliery on the same footing as other collieries.

After a meeting between manager and men, the lodge informed Wilson that they were deferring a decision to 24 February. The manager replied two days later with an ultimatum:

> Unless you are prepared to meet me, on or before Monday the 11th instant, the offer made to you will be withdrawn and other necessary steps will be taken to effect essential reductions.

The Dawdon men refused to budge, and at this point Londonderry's agents took a provocative step which they hoped would involve the Durham Agents. The lodge was anxious not to involve their leaders as they knew that Peter Lee was in favour of accepting reductions rather than risking industrial action. On 15 February notices were posted to the effect that the men would be locked out from 2 March. The management's intentions are clear from an internal letter written by Londonderry's agents:

> It is probable that the Durham Agents will now take the matter in hand and I am of the opinion that we should ask that piece workers be reduced to, say, 25 per cent above the county average. Houses in turn should be abolished [the practice of issuing colliery houses on a rota basis].

Starting to put and hew should be abolished. Cavils should be put in every six months instead of every 12 weeks as at present. I shall be obliged for your view and instructions on this matter.

However, the Durham Agents had not been contacted by the lodge, and the lockout of 3,800 men duly took place on 2 March. It was 10 March before a meeting between management and men took place and only after this meeting that Richardson, one of the DMA Agents,was called in. The Durham executive recommended that the lodge accept the new terms of employment offered, but when put to a ballot of the men they rejected these terms by 1,052 votes to 752.

Under pressure, the lodge officials decided to accept the recommendation from Durham and called a meeting to which the DMA executive was invited, after which another ballot was organised. To their surprise, the majority against acceptance actually increased and Londonderry began to sit up and take notice. Having previously refused to be directly involved, he now met with area officials and modified his demands, saying that if the men would accept the piece-rate reductions then the special payments for hitches could go to arbitration. The DMA regarded these terms as better than at any pit in County Durham, but this clearly did not impress the locked-out men. This time the majority against acceptance was even bigger (1,221 to 727)

WIR kitchen Dawdon 1929   *Photo Ancrum collection*

Politics were undoubtedly having an effect on the dispute. Ramsay MacDonald had been adopted as the Labour candidate for the Seaham constituency, replacing Sidney Webb, who retired. Ramsay MacDonald was a personal friend of Londonderry, a fact which he had, on the advice of Webb, studiously avoided telling the Dawdon miners. Not only did he continue to visit Londonderry at Wynyard Hall but he had an affair with the good lord's wife.

Also active in the constituency was the Communist Party which, under the direction of Moscow, was pursuing a line of total opposition to trade union and Labour Party leaders. This 'left' phase in the history of the Communist Party became known as the 'Third Period', involving a series of twists and turns in policy from left to right which lasted for another decade and resulted in the Hitler-Stalin pact.

The Communist Party intervened in the Dawdon dispute through the International Workers' Relief (IWR), an organisation set up by the Communist International to organise material solidarity to workers on strike. IWR sent James Ancrum, a Communist Party councillor from Felling, to organise a kitchen to provide meals for Dawdon miners' families. Despite the combined efforts of management and union to prevent Ancrum from hiring a suitable hall, the kitchen was successfully

James Ancrum

organised and did great service. This practical help must have gained the party some respect as a May Day demonstration in Dawdon addressed by Ancrum and Party leader Harry Pollitt was attended by 2,000 people.

Ramsay MacDonald was asked by the lodge to

appoint an intermediary to try and break the deadlock, and nominated WL Cook of the government's Mines Department. This led to a virtual re-offer of what had previously been agreed with the Durham Agents, except that hitch differences not resolved were to be settled by arbitration. Not risking another ballot defeat, the officials took a vote on a show of hands, and it was decided to return to work on 13 July and put outstanding issues to arbitration.

But the fat was soon in the fire once again. So deeply did the Dawdon men now distrust their officials that they nominated three men to represent them at arbitration: AJ Cook, the MFGB secretary, Harry Pollitt, leader of the Communist Party, and George Lumley, communist checkweighman at Ryhope. Though coming second in the vote, it was Lumley who was finally chosen to represented the men. Lumley was immovable in his refusal to accept any worsening of conditions whatsoever, causing great exasperation all round, including to Ramsay MacDonald, who wrote to one of the Durham officials:

> I cannot conceal from you my quiet concern about the way that your affairs are being handled by a communist of the type of Lumley. Lumley can no more effect a settlement than my boot can, nor has he any intention of doing so. . . . Can you do something to clear Lumley out on account of his incompetence? If you would face him up to the hard facts of failure to do anything, things would begin to get done.

Lumley and the Dawdon men held firm well into the autumn. On 3 October the employers gave one week's notice that they would close the pit. The Durham officials declared that if this second lockout came about there would be no strike pay, in this way forcing the Dawdon men to accept the appointment of an independent umpire.

The umpire, the Department of Mines' Sir Harold Morris, ruled that the owners' offer be accepted, and on 4 November the men reluctantly agreed to the terms on offer.

In the general election of 1929 the Labour Party gained more seats than the other parties but failed to gain an overall majority. MacDonald formed the second Labour administration dependent on the support of the Liberal Party. If the miners of Durham had high hopes from this administration they were to be bitterly disappointed.

After the Wall Street crash of 1929 the world economy was plunged into a desperate slump. Under pressure from the banks MacDonald introduced the hated Means Test and reduced the dole. These measures split the Cabinet and the Labour government collapsed. MacDonald then formed a National Government dominated by

Tories, and made his old friend Londonderry Secretary of State for Air, a post which he held until 1935.

In the election held on 27 October 1931, MacDonald stood against the Labour candidate, W Coxon, in Seaham and held his seat with a reduced majority of 6,000. George Lumley, who was then a member of the DMA executive committee, invited the wrath of the Durham Agents by standing in the election as the Communist candidate, thus opposing the official DMA nominee, Coxon. As a result, Lumley will forever occupy a special place in history as the only Durham miner to stand in election against a prime minister.

The great depression of the 1930s had an immediate effect in Durham. In May 1924 Durham's collieries employed 172,026 miners. By December 1931 this figure had plummeted to 107,938, many of whom were on short-time working. No colliery, however efficient, avoided the slump in the export trade. Londonderry collieries dismissed 2,600 men between 1931 and 1932. The collieries in the west were particularly hard hit, a great number closing down completely. In many villages there was 100-per-cent unemployment and in 1934 the rate of unemployment amongst insured workers in the Bishop Auckland Area was 50.4 per cent, against a national average of 16.1 per cent. Miners at those pits which were working short time could not claim benefit unless they had three consecutive days without employment. The Means Test required that a household claiming relief must have no saleable assets and nobody earning. The men from the Assistance Board could visit a house and compel the family to sell household goods such as clocks, cushions, pillow cases and sheets before allowing benefit. A son or daughter who

Unemployed protest 1930s Felling   *Ancrum collection*

Sam Watson, who was known as an intelligent and well-read miner with communist sympathies. He had written a widely acclaimed pamphlet which informed miners of their rights when claiming assistance. Although he had never served on the Durham executive he had a powerful friend in Red Hills, Will Lawther, who supported him in 1936 and helped his election to the position of Durham Agent.

had a job disqualified the parents from benefit. Working sons often moved out of the house and slept rough rather than disqualify their parents and across the county shanty towns developed where single men and evicted families lived.

On 12 September 1932 the Durham Public Assistance Committee refused to implement the Means Test. They were supported by the County Council and the government was forced to appoint a commissioner to administer the scheme.

The DMA ran a campaign against the harsh treatment of the unemployed which brought to the fore the secretary of Boldon Miners' Lodge,

By 1935 the Labour Party had recovered to some extent from the betrayal of 1931 and Emmanuel Shinwell won back the Seaham seat for Labour with a majority of 21,000 votes.

Londonderry pursued his political career in other directions and became a personal friend of Hitler, whom he was fond of visiting. He was so enthusiastic about the developments in Germany that he wrote a Penguin Special entitled *Ourselves and Germany,* arguing that it was in Britain's

Londonderry and Hitler

interests to extend a hand of friendship to Hitler. Less than a decade later, when the Russian army took Berlin, they found his little book in Hitler's bunker, bearing the author's inscription:

To the Fuhrer with my best wishes and the most serious hope for the best and most long lasting mutual understanding between our two countries.

No issue produced more anger in the coalfields in the 1930s than that of company unionism, represented by the breakaway 'non-political union' led by GA Spencer, who claimed that 10,000 miners in Durham, 6 per cent of all miners in the county, were in his union immediately after the 1926 dispute. By 1936 most had rejoined the DMA.

GA Spencer MP represented the Nottinghamshire miners and was to go down in history as the one who did his level best to smash that unity and 'break the Federation'.

In October 1926, when Durham and the main coalfields voted to reject the government's terms for a return to work, Spencer had approached the Nottingham employers for separate terms, for a return to work with a reduction in wages. This occasioned AJ Cook to say to the delegates at a subsequent conference:

'I hope this conference will treat Mr Spencer as a blackleg. Mr Spencer is a blackleg of the worst order.' And chairman Herbert Smith told him: 'I would rather be shot in the morning than do what you have done.'

Spencer and the other Nottingham delegates were

Ryhope strike-breakers being escorted home during 16 week strike against reductions, 1932
Photo: Sunderland Echo

ordered out of the special conference and were suspended.

In November 1926 Spencer formed a 'non-political union', the Nottinghamshire and District Miners' Industrial Union, later to be called Miners' Industrial (non-political) Union. Not unexpectedly, the employers gave considerable assistance to Spencer, giving preferential treatment to members of his organisation over those belonging to the MFGB. At Hucknall colliery in Nottinghamshire only Spencer's men were employed. For many months there were conflicts and clashes, especially in South Wales. At Chopwell colliery the owners tried to make a separate agreement with two hundred men who were in the 'non-political union' but were thwarted when the DMA lodge took the Consett

Coal Company to court and won their case.

In 1935 the conflict with Spencer's union intensified. At every turn Spencer and his organisation hampered the wages campaign. The Nottinghamshire Miners' Union (NMA) represented those miners who remained loyal to the MFGB, but it was not recognised by the owners and thousands of Nottinghamshire miners were deprived of the freedom to be represented by a union of their choice. In many cases the owners made it a condition of employment that a levy for Spencer's union was deducted from weekly wages.

By 1936 Spencer's failure to fight the employers eroded support for his union and more and more miners joined the NMA, increasing tension across the coalfield. The smouldering discontent burst into flames in August 1936 at Harworth colliery, one of six Nottinghamshire pits owned by Barber, Walker and Co., when two boys employed as colliers were physically assaulted by a colliery official. This caused great anger.

The majority of Harworth workers were members of the NMA, which sought a meeting with the management, who refused, saying they would only talk to the company union.

Two weeks later, a majority of men stopped work when two men were sacked for taking their 'snap time' without the permission of a depty.

When the NMA asked for a meeting they were told this could happen only if there was a return to work, which the men agreed to do. However, the manager now inflamed the situation once again by seeking to punish those whom he called the ringleaders of the strike, insisting on certain signed conditions before they could return. The men demanded a strike ballot and the MFGB took over responsibility for handling the dispute. They advised the men to hold a pit-head ballot to determine which union the miners wanted to represent them at the pit, after which 'if thought advisable' notices should be handed in.

Seeking to settle the dispute by negotiation, the federation wrote to the owners for a meeting and got the usual reply: 'My directors have complete confidence in the management, and therefore no good purpose would be served by a personal interview.' Another failed attempt prompted the federation to refer the question to the Department of Mines, who in turn also got short shrift from the owners.

It was clear that a major strike was now in the offing, and the MFGB took the decision to pay any men who lost their unemployment benefit as a result of the strike. They also advised the men to withhold their notices and take part in a ballot.

This ballot produced the expected result:

For the Nottinghamshire Miners Association and the Mineworkers' Federation: 1,175
For the 'industrial union': 145 - Majority: 1,030.

On this basis it was decided to hand in strike notices for 23 November. In fact the strike started six days earlier, because the men were already out on a checkweigh dispute and rejected advice to return.

also threatening to turn the men and women out of their houses.

At a special delegate conference Arthur Horner spoke, 'asking the conference for power, without waiting for any further conference, to take a ballot of the British miners in order that we may start a national strike, if necessary, to obtain freedom for the Nottinghamshire miners'. Others, including JE Swan, Durham delegate, spoke in strong support, and the vote was unanimous.

The federation called for a national levy to support the Harworth men and the response surpassed all expectations. It was clear that the issues at stake were being taken extremely seriously.

A small number of men continued to work and there were clashes between police and miners. Six men were imprisoned, and eight fined varying sums from £1 to £5. The owners were

Ryhope strike-breakers being escorted to work 1932

Opinion nationally was greatly influenced by the report of the National Council for Civil Liberties, exposing 'serious irregularities in the conduct of the police', and declaring:

> It is unfortunate that so much of the public administration of the county is in the hands of those whose economic interests coincide with the interests of the owners rather than with the interests of the men who are dependent on the owners for their livelihood.

Ronald Kidd also stated bluntly in his report that 'the village is practically owned by the company', and noted: 'I am satisfied that the company have used their economic power to deprive the men of their civil right of freedom of assembly.'

The government's Secretary for Mines invited the MFGB to meet with representatives of Spencer's organisation, with a view to discussing the prospect of settling the dispute on the basis of amalgamation of the two unions. The MFGB replied that if this could be done on reasonable terms they had no objection, and the meeting took place on 25 February. In a series of meetings, agreement was reached on the terms of an amalgamation, but neither Spencer nor the company would budge on the question of a satisfactory settlement of the Harworth dispute itself.

When a special conference met on the first two days of April, the proposed terms for amalgamation received strong criticism. Swan from Durham, who said 'nobody would call me a left-wing man', condemned them as 'obnoxious'. The executive, responding to this mood, recommended to conference a national strike ballot, and this was carried by 503 votes to 32.

The ballot result was overwhelming: 444,546 for strike, and 61,445 against; in Durham, 70,337 for and 11,668 against; 98.9 per cent of British miners had voted! It seemed that with this level of support for a national strike the MFGB was poised to smash Spencerism once and for all.

The situation in Harworth was now extremely tense, with daily confrontations and clashes. On 29 April, thirty-six persons were summoned for unlawful assembly to disturb the public peace and 'making a great riot and disturbance'. The defence lawyer Stafford Cripps demonstrated in court that many of those charged had been indiscriminately arrested and that there was no evidence of their having been present at the disturbance. Most of the defendants were acquitted or given very light sentences, but seventeen were sent for trial at Nottingham Assizes.

The executive, through the offices of the Department of Mines, sought again to find a settlement without strike action. After more stubborn refusals by the owners, it was eventually found possible to renew the idea of an amalgamation, and the executive put this to the recalled special conference. It was rejected. When Will Lawther moved the recommendation, Durham delegate J Newman shouted:

We have come here for one thing, the only way to get rid of Spencer. What are we afraid of? We have decided unanimously in this country for notices to be handed in. Carry out the dictates of the country and dispose of Spencer.

After others spoke in the same vein, the recommendation was turned down by 343 votes to 192. The executive made an unprecedented criticism of the delegates but had to now issue a clarion call 'to the mineworkers of Britain!', including the words:

'We ask you to hand in your notices, and let these men see, beyond the possibility of doubt, that the miners are invincibly determined to fight for justice. . . .

'With a full sense of our responsibility, and with a clear understanding of what may lie before us all, we urge you to take this action , because we believe that the principles of freedom, justice

Arthur Horner (left) and Will Lawther, before the meeting with owners and the Ministry, March 8, 1944

and democracy, which we are now seeking to establish in Nottingham, are worthy of fighting for to the limits of our strength.'

Once again the coalfields were poised for action. Never had the MFGB membership been so united.

The National Government and its Prime Minister Baldwin were in serious trouble. As the MFGB delegates set off home to the coalfields to organise the strike, 26,000 busmen in London struck work seeking a seven-and-a-half hour day. The coronation of King George VI was to take place on 12 May. With the miners threatening the biggest strike since 1926 all Baldwin's careful preparations to unite the country in the celebration of a new king seemed doomed.

On 5 May Baldwin made a passionate plea in the name of patriotism to 'that handful of men with whom rests peace or war' to 'rend and dissipate this dark cloud which has gathered over us'.

Page Arnot reminds us in his history of the Miners' Federation that these were words from the same Baldwin 'who had broadcast to the American public in 1926 asking them not to send food to the starving miners as it would only prolong the struggle, and who had been responsible for the anti-trade union legislation of 1927.'

Next day the MFGB executive, in direct response to Baldwin's plea, suspended the strike notices for a further two weeks and continued their discussions with the department of mines.

However, the other parties, Spencer and the owners, were less moved by Baldwin and refused an 'unconditional' meeting. Again a week's grace was given by the executive to allow further efforts. Sensing that the MFGB was vacillating, Spencer and the owners again rejected the invitation of the Secretary of Mines.

Now the strike seemed truly unavoidable, and a definite date, 29 May, was fixed for notices to be handed in. There followed a frantic round of activity by the Department of Mines, which, together with a surge of popular support for the

Mick Kane, Chairman Harworth Branch, on release from imprisonment

MFGB's cause, brought about a change. The MFGB executive gave its subcommittee 'full powers to negotiate terms of fusion', and called a special conference for 27 May, two days before the strike was due. By the time of the conference,

MEMORIAL MEETING
IN HONOUR
of the NORTH EAST MEN of the
BRITISH BATTALION
who laid down their Lives in Spain.

Coun. BOB ELLIOTT.

IN THE

CITY HALL
NEWCASTLE upon TYNE

SUNDAY, 15th. JANUARY, 1939.

at 7.30 p.m.   Doors open at 7 p.m.

CLIFF LAWTHER.

Speakers—

Sir CHARLES TREVELYAN,

WILL LAWTHER, (M.F.G.B.)

HAMILTON FYFE,

F. M. GRAHAM, (British Battalion)

JOHN GOSS of London, will Sing.

WILF JOBLING.

Supported by :—

Miss ELLEN WILKINSON, M.P.	DAVID ADAMS, M.P.	WILLIAM WHITELY, M.P.
J. CHUTER EDE, M.P.	J. J. LAWSON, M.P.	SAM WATSON, Agent D.M.A

LYALL WILKES, Prospective Labour Candidate, Central Division, Newcastle.
ARTHUR BLENKINSOP, Prospective Labour Candidate, East Division, Newcastle.

JAMES BOWMAN, Sec., N.M.A	Coun. WM. ALLAN.	Miss ENID ATKINSON.
	WILLIAM HEPPLE, (A.E.U.)	

24 men from the North East were killed in Spain in 1936 fighting Fascism amongst them was Blaydon miner Cliff Lawther brother of Will Lawther the executive had received a report of a meeting between the two sides, and reported to the conference that it was now possible to recommend an agreed settlement on fusion.

The terms of the agreement were that the two organisations in Nottinghamshire amalgamate into a single union, called the Nottinghamshire and District Miners' Federated Union, to be affiliated to the MFGB. Spencer was to be president and MFGB executive committee member, the other offices being shared. There was a general commitment for the reinstatement of the Harworth men.

The 350 men needed at Harworth would be taken on in an order decided by the drawing of lots. With this agreed, the six-month strike was called off.

Four weeks after the return to work, Mick Kane, chairman of the Harworth NMA branch, and sixteen other Harworth miners appeared at Nottingham Assizes and were sentenced as follows:

Michael Kane: two years; Chandler and JH Smith: fifteen months; Carney: twelve months; Barker, Jobson, Murray, Wilson, Risdale and Mrs.

Margaret Haymer: nine months; T. Smith: six months; Richardson: four months.

Five others were acquitted.

War years

The declaration of war in 1939 did not bring immediate relief to the depressed villages of the Durham coalfield. The disruption of the sea links between the North East and London made the trade situation worse. Miners, both unemployed and in work, saw their chance to escape from the rigours of the mining industry and 16,000 joined the forces or found other jobs. This did not eliminate the problem. In September 1939 there were 18,372 miners unemployed in Durham. By December the figure had been reduced only to 15,087, and in March 1940 there were still 6,571 unemployed.

A ridiculous situation arose when miners agreed to double-shift working and the suspension of statutory holidays to boost production. The difficulties of transporting the coal out of the region and the loss of markets on the Continent meant that the increased production led to short-time working and unemployment. So severe was the problem that the DMA even contemplated resettling Durham miners in other coalfields.

In May 1941 the government introduced the Essential Work (Coal Mining Industry) Order (EWO), making coalmining a reserved occupation. Under this order miners were not allowed to leave the industry or even change pits and striking and absenteeism were illegal.

The chaos of the first year of the war now led to a labour shortage and the government appealed for volunteers to man the pits. Durham's Regional Coal Controller asked for 5,000 volunteers between the ages of 18 and 25 to come forward. Only 180 answered the call. By December 1943 the situation was desperate and young men were directed into the mines when called up. These Bevin Boys, as they became known, were recruited from all parts of Britain and from all occupations. By the end of the war there were 6,900 working in Durham's pits.

Miners who had suffered decades of poverty and unemployment found themselves working under the military discipline of the EWO. However, this did not prevent them fighting for their rights. During the war years there were over 200 reported stoppages in Durham's mines. Although they were invariably strikes of short duration, they evoked the wrath of the government, and also that of the DMA.

The miners of Wearmouth colliery were criticised for insisting that they were brought to bank during the heavy air raids which the port of Sunderland suffered throughout the war. The miners argued that the close proximity of the pit to the main target of the bombers, the shipyards, made Wearmouth colliery more vulnerable than other mines. One direct hit in the shaft area could cause a disaster of enormous proportions.

On 18 November 1943 the *Northern Echo* published a statement issued by the executive of the DMA:

> The reckless stoppages are not a manifestation of the high standard of valour and the testing qualities of grit for which the Durham miners have been renowned. They are a violation of pledges and can only be designated consciously or otherwise as sabotaging the war effort and assisting the enemy.

A miner and ex-soldier replied to the statement in the same newspaper:

> If I had not known who had issued the DMA circular I would have blamed the coal owners. I fail to find one word in the circular about the coal owners being to blame for some of these reckless stoppages. With reference to the miners letting our lads down who are fighting in Italy, if the lads who are doing the fighting knew the wages and conditions we miners are still undergoing they would surely ask themselves what they are fighting for?

On 26 June 1942, thirteen men died in an explosion in the Five Quarter Back Over flat at Murton colliery.

In 1944 the MFGB consisted of a federation of forty-one autonomous unions organised in twenty areas. Throughout the war the MFGB had attempted to reach agreement to rationalise the organisation into more manageable areas and seek amalgamations which would eventually lead to a national union.

On 16 August 1944 a special conference was held to draw up the objects of a new union, the National Union of Mineworkers. Among the resolutions was one Durham resolution which proposed that the union objective was: 'to seek the establishment of public ownership and control of the mining industry'.

The National Union of Mineworkers was brought into existence on 1 January 1945. In May of that year the Second World War ended and in July the first Labour government with an overall majority was elected.

Gala 1940s

Wearmouth miners' Lodge committee on Vesting day 1947

Chapter 8

Vesting Day, 1 January 1947, the day the mining industry passed from private ownership to state ownership. Expectations were high. The coal owners, who had ruled the lives of thousands upon thousands of miners' families for generations, ceased to rule. The newly established Northern Divisional Coal Board (Durham, Northumberland and Cumberland) became responsible overnight for more than 200 pits and attached workings, together with 44,000 colliery houses, 200 firms, 100,000 acres of land, 18 coking plants in Durham, several brickworks, over 100 local electricity systems and 'miscellaneous items including a mortuary, a fish-and-chip shop and a public house'.

Vesting Day was celebrated by virtually every mining community in Durham with dances and socials. Parades to the pit-heads were organised, and the blue-and-white flag of the National Coal Board (NCB) was unfurled and flown from the highest point on the headgear. The entrance to each pit was marked by a notice board:

Raising the flag Vesting day Easington colliery

THIS COLLIERY IS NOW MANAGED BY THE NATIONAL COAL BOARD ON BEHALF OF THE PEOPLE

Fathers carrying their children on their shoulders told them: 'All of this now belongs to us.' The National Union of Mineworkers greeted the change with enthusiasm. Speaking to conference delegates before Vesting Day, NUM General Secretary Arthur Horner said:

> We must take a long view, because the advancement of our members' interests lies not in sneaking victories from coal owners, but in establishing a firm and highly productive

industry out of which these things can come and continue to come for ever and ever. That is a different role for our members.

Horner continued in the same vein, telling delegates that 'the day of agitation for campaigning for these things is nearly finished', and:

> The task in future is to use the best means we know to fight Mother Nature and to drag the coal out of her bosom. The future that lies before us is tremendous. The pits are ours. We can say what can be done with them.

Some delegates were less sanguine, to say the

least, pointing to the names and records of those appointed to run the National Coal Board, including Chairman Lord Hyndley, ex-boss of Powell Duffryn and Co., major coalowners. Also appointed to the Board was Ebby Edwards, who resigned as secretary of the NUM to take his seat, and Lord Citrine, who had been the secretary of the TUC when the general strike was called off in 1926. Even Tory Harold Macmillan was shrewd enough to comment, tongue in cheek, on this appointment in the debate in the House of Commons:

> May not the miner, remembering Keir Hardie, Bob Smillie and Herbert Smith, all those great figures of the old great days, and contemplating Lord Hyndley, echo Milton's words and say: 'New Presbyter is but old Priest writ large'?

The miners' lodge at St Hilda's colliery, South Shields, agreed. They refused to take part in the Vesting Day celebrations saying: 'It [Nationalisation] is just a different play with the same old actors.' Marsden Miners' Lodge came to the same conclusion and boycotted the Vesting Day celebrations.

A further bone of contention occurred when the level of compensation was announced. The miners' union had started the campaign for nationalisation as long ago as 1906 and Bob Smillie had never tired of insisting that no compensation should be paid to the owners.

A total of £165 million was paid for collieries, and royalty owners were given £78 million, a true king's ransom in the currency values of 1947. As a further sweetener, the coal owners were given government stock in the form of annuities which would be paid to them until the year 2000!

For many decades, every miner worked a part of every working day to pay the interest on the

Sam Watson

money borrowed to pay this compensation. Sam Watson, however, was upbeat when he declared on Vesting Day:

> Our industry is now publicly owned. No longer are we working for colliery owners. No longer are profits being paid to absentee owners. No longer is it 'They and Them', it is 'We and Us'. The industry has passed from the propaganda stage to the administrative stage, and in place of political theorising, slogans and alibis we have to put good, sound planning, real hard work based upon maximum co-operation and efficiency, and sound thinking reinforced with the acceptance of individual responsibility and self-discipline, combining all three in a concerted effort to improve the productivity of our industry.

After the war the country was plunged into a huge coal crisis and the miners were needed more than ever before. But if miners thought that this would mean the immediate granting of 'The Miners Charter' drawn up by the NUM prior to nationalisation they were to be disappointed. The new board refused to give miners a national standard wage, a second week's paid holiday, compensation for industrial diseases, or a seven-hour shift.

In May a five-day-week agreement was concluded but miners were asked to continue to work Saturdays until the coal crisis abated. Even the Essential Work Order was kept in place. Miners worked on in hope that things would change.

At some collieries there was little pretence that things had changed. Stan Pierce started work as a miner in the last six months of private ownership at the Glebe colliery, Washington. He recalled:

> On vesting day I was 14 and the youngest person working at the mine and I was sent for. They didn't tell me anything about it. I was just sent for. The oldest member of the pit, he was sent for. They had a plaque saying that the pit was now owned by the people and the colliery manager unveiled it. Then we were sent home. It was nowt flash. At some pits the men were given a memento but we got nowt like that.

> The first boss we got under nationalisation was Major Barron, who had been a Major in the Indian Army and he thought he could treat us the way he treated the Indians over there. He had this bad manner and he caused more strikes than enough at the Glebe.

> He would go in-bye and antagonise the men. He caused one strike 'cos he was paying men shift work when they were hewing coal. All the men got taken to court because the war-time restrictions were still on then. They all got bound over and were told that if they did it again they would go to jail. It didn't make any difference 'cos the men would walk out at the drop of a hat.

> He always tried to 'divide and rule'. He had a number one set of hewers and a number two set of hewers. One team were the big hewers the

Above: Tanfield Lea lodge, Stanley returning from Gala 1940s

Left: Concessionary coal in back lane Tanfield Lea , Stanley 1940s

Photos: Gerald R Ash

Above deputies trip Tanfield Lea 1940s

Left: Tanfield Lea Miners lodge committee

Photos: Gerald R Ash

other team was the spiv shift. That was the crack.

I'll never forget one time when two pufflers from two teams of hewers went to see him about a dispute. When they come out the meeting they were both deputies. I'll never forget that, one of them became a first shift overman and the other ended up a dowty counter. They were never really forgiven for that. Anyone who went into a deputation after that was always warned not to come back as deputies.

There was always trouble about the laying-out fines. The weighman would say: 'Lay out that tub'. Well there might have been four tubs up against the 'keps' waiting to go into the tippler and they were always getting the wrong tub. There was hell on.

Miners underground

Although many things remained the same there were also big changes. Many of the larger pits in the east of the county had pit-head baths built just before the war. The first was at Boldon colliery in 1922. In the west of the county very few had pit-head baths. A major programme was initiated for building baths and canteens. Soon these brick-built facilities with steel window-frames were a familiar sight throughout the coalfield.

The management culture on safety was harder to reverse. Only eight months after nationalisation, a roof-fall at Whitehaven colliery, Cumberland, killed 107 men on 17 August 1947. One week later twenty-one men were killed in an explosion at Louisa Old pit, Stanley, County Durham.

For the first three years of nationalisation coal was at a premium and there was a general increase in piece-rate earnings. At the onset of the new decade miners at the coal face were reaping the rewards of decades of struggle. New training schemes were initiated and residential training schools were opened at Easington, New Kyo, and Washington.

Jacky McCowliff started work in 1952 at Hylton colliery. After nine months working on the screens at bank he was sent to Usworth colliery to do his underground training for sixteen weeks. Others went to the new residential training school at Dame Margaret's Hall, Washington, near the Glebe colliery.

Back at the pit he spent a month underground under close personal supervision (CPS). He worked in the shaft area for a year working three shifts, 4a.m., 11a.m. and 7p.m., before moving in-bye to the 'clippers' up the North West drift to an area of the Hutton seam. He recalled:

> You started working in the landing and worked your way in-bye to the face and coal hewing. I was putting off the fillers when I was 17. We were right next to the coal face but we had to have coal-face training to go on to the face.
>
> I had to do a year's coal-face training at Ryhope colliery, so before I got on the face hewing I was 20 years old. To become fully 'face efficient'

you had to do another 20 days' coal cutting.

Hewers, fillers and pullers at Hylton were making good money, sometimes as much as £11 to £16 a week. Mind, every penny that was made was haggled over with the deputies and as far as the under-manager or even the manager. Nine times out of ten we come to good agreements.

The constant disputes which the piece work system produced continued to dog the industry. At most collieries each team of men had chosen one of their number to act as a puffler. Jacky McCowliff recalled:

> We had pufflers to make sure we had been paid right. On a Thursday the puffler would get the master note with all the men's earnings on. He

Hewer in thin seam

Chilton lodge, setting out for Gala 1940s

went through it making sure that all the considerations, all the waiting-on, and all of that had been entered in. If it wasn't right when they got down the pit they would go to the 'kist' and all the men would be there arguing about it. If the note was wrong they would pull up the deputy. Then we had a number one deputy and a number two deputy and if they couldn't agree the puffler would see the overman. If he didn't sort it out he'd turn around and come out-bye and his men would do his filling for him. He was allowed to do this and come back down the

pit. If he didn't get any success I've seen times when the pufflers rang in-bye and told the men and they've walked off the face and went home. It didn't happen that often at Hylton but the men would do it.

Whatever the problems of the post-war years there was a definite feeling of optimism throughout the colliery communities, a definite feeling that the dark days of the 1920s and 1930s were now irrevocably behind them. Nowhere was this feeling reflected more than at the Big Meeting where the atmosphere reflected a new sense of celebration. Children danced in front of the bands and outside the County Hotel, proudly chanting the name of their village. Men rolled up their trouser-legs and turned jackets inside out, the stripes on the lining providing a little gaiety in what was still a black-and-white world.

The early 1950s were not all happy times. On 30 May 1951 an explosion at Easington colliery caused the death of 83 men, two of whom were from the rescue brigade. While the county was reeling from this tragedy another explosion at Eppleton colliery claimed the lives of nine men in July.

Before nationalisation there were thirty-seven different rescue stations in the country administered by thirty-one separate bodies. The NCB organised them all under one body, which greatly improved their efficiency. In the North East the rescue stations were situated in Houghton-le-Spring in East Durham, Crook in West Durham, Benwell Towers in South Northumberland, and Ashington in North Northumberland. Each covered the pits in their immediate vicinity and then called upon the closest to assist if necessary. In addition each pit had its own part-time rescue brigade drawn from volunteers. It is a testimony to the character of

miners that there was no shortage of volunteers and at every pit there was intense competition to become one of the rescue brigade. At Easington hundreds of these men battled their way to reach the victims and two tragically fell pray to the poisonous gas.

Immediately the fuel crisis was over, pits started to close. In 1949 four pits and drifts at Burnhope closed with the loss of 779 jobs, 501 when Hetton Lyons closed in 1950, and 277 when Axwell Park closed in 1951. Only those involved noticed these closures in a county which still had over 130 mines employing over 120,000 men, a quarter of the male population.

The future for coal looked bright and millions of pounds were invested in the bigger pits to the east

Coffins of Easington victims prepared for burial

Rescue brigadesmen

Durham Miners' Gala 1950

and some of the mid-Durham mines. In 1952 a new shaft was sunk at Murton to become the coal-drawing shaft of an enormous underground complex linking Elemore, Eppleton and Murton. All the big collieries sunk on the east coast were transformed by this investment into super-pits.

The coalfield divided into three distinctive parts: the west, the east and mid-Durham. In the west the seams were thin and hard to work by modern mining techniques, but the coal was of high quality and coking coal. Its increased selling price offset the cost of production and while coking coal was in demand these collieries were safe.

In the central corridor the pits were older than those in the east and the coal was not of the quality of that in the west. They were also prone to flooding.

In the east, under the limestone, the coal was thick and continued out under the North Sea, but no one knew how far. To find out, the NCB began to sink boreholes from offshore rigs throughout the late 1950s and 1960s. The results were good and it was calculated that there was enough coal to keep the coastal pits open for 200 years.

By 1965 cheap oil was flooding into the country and it became apparent that the NCB was determined to close what it deemed to be less efficient pits. Between 1960 and 1965, apart from

Easington banner at Gala, after disaster, 1951

one or two exceptions, the pits which closed were the smaller units, many of which were drift mines. In the second half of the decade the coalfield was decimated.

Shearer at Murton colliery

It was generally believed that most of the closures were due to exhaustion but the NCB's own figures show that in the west of the county by 1962 only 127.2 million tons had been worked out of 592 million tons which was available.

Up until 1969 there had been no county-wide strikes in Durham and no national strike of miners since 1926: forty-three years of relative industrial peace. Of course the day-to-day disputes over piece-work continued, but when there was a walk-out it often involved only part of the workforce. Putters or hewers would have a dispute in one district and walk out for a few days and return when an agreement had been reached.

Mechanisation of the industry created methods of coal production which were unsuitable for the operation of piece-work. As the 1960s progressed, more and more coal was extracted at the face by machinery, filled on to belts mechanically, and transported to bank either in new 2-ton mine cars or on conveyer belts. It was no longer the brute strength of the miner but the reliability of machines that determined how much coal was produced. In 1966 the NCB negotiated a National Power Loading Agreement (NPLA) which standardised rates of pay for each class of workmen. Although there were variations between areas, the NPLA became a strong unifying force within the NUM.

Under the leadership of Sam Watson, the Durham area developed a reputation for moderation. After his election as an agent in 1936, Watson gravitated away from the communist sympathies he had harboured as a young lodge official towards the right wing of the Labour Party. He believed that the role of the union was to create an efficient and profitable industry and that it was in the long-term interests of miners to make sacrifices. He believed in training a whole generation of miners in these ideas. His classes at Red Hills for young miners became known as Sam Watson's Sunday School. When he retired in 1963 he handed over a union whose agents were all schooled in the

Wingate Grange colliery, day of closure 15 August 1962
Photo: Margaret Crossley (her father William Crossley is the miner 4th from left in back row)

Silksworth colliery 1960s   *Photo: Sunderland Echo*

Whitburn colliery 1960s   *Photo: Sunderland Echo*

tradition of moderation and co-operation.

The Sam Watson school of thought was prevalent on the national executive of the NUM, which Watson had dominated for many years. In 1965, two years after Watson retired, the NUM came to an agreement with the Labour government to write off the £415 million debt which the industry had accrued, mostly due to the compensation paid to the former owners. In exchange the NUM agreed not to oppose the closure of the unprofitable units. Between 1965 and 1969, two hundred pits were closed throughout the country, a rate of one a week. A disproportionate number of these collieries, 57 in all, were in Durham.

Alf Hesler, who succeeded Watson, reflected the general views of the Durham agents when he said:

Sam Watson's Sunday School, Chairman of NCB Alf Robens, centre

We as a union must concentrate our efforts on securing the introduction of new industries in the area to absorb our members, and while it is sad to see the decline in membership in our great union, as an ex-miner myself, I say in all sincerity, that there are many more congenial ways of earning a living than toiling in the mines.

Last shift, Washington F pit, 1978   Photo: Sunderland Echo

The Labour government helped create some alternative employment when it announced in 1967 that the new power station to be built at Hartlepool, almost in sight of the South Durham super-pits, was to be powered by nuclear energy. Years later Harold Wilson admitted in private that this decision was a deliberate attempt to give Durham miners the message that coal was finished.

Not all lodges followed the Sam Watson school of thought. Whitburn colliery and Ryhope, in particular, were noted for their militancy and ability to confront management.

Ryhope was closed in 1966 and Whitburn in 1968. Both these collieries were surrounded by massive coal reserves and Ryhope had been modernised at a cost of over £1 million.

Vane Tempest, Murton and Wearmouth all mined coal within the Ryhope take for many years after the closure. Not surprisingly, those on the left suspected that these

Deputies and their families Gala 1960s

lodges were closed because of their militant stance.

Towards the end of the 1960s, the productivity of British coal-face workers had risen from 58.4 cwt per man-shift in 1947 to 137.7 cwt per man-shift in 1969. In 1948 miners were earning 29 per cent above the national average for manufacturing. By 1970 they were earning 3.1 per cent below the national average. After 23 years of nationalisation British miners had lost close to half-a-million jobs and slipped well down the earnings league. However, under nationalisation a new workforce had developed whose memory did not stretch back to the defeat of 1926. The old miners' lament, 'striking gets you nowhere', was heard less and less on the coalfield.

Because the average wage in the industry had slumped below the national average, those on the lowest pay were experiencing real hardship. Barry Chambers who became the Blackhall lodge secretary remembered: 'The lads who were travellers started to complain that the bus driver who drove them to the pit was earning more money than they were.'

Surface workers were particularly badly paid and they were still working a forty-one-and-a-quarter-hour week. Although many resolutions had been carried at national conference calling for a seven-and-three-quarter-hour shift for surface workers, nothing had been done. On Monday 13 October 1969, the Yorkshire Area took strike action, demanding a shorter shift for surfacemen. During that week pickets appeared outside Durham collieries. Jacky McCowliff remembered:

> We went down the pit in back shift and we got word that Westoe men had gone on strike over the eight hours for banksmen. We heard that Westoe men were at the gates and we expected to be called out. I was surprised that the night shift men came down and when we were passing them they confirmed that there were Westoe men at the gates.

> At Hylton there was a long road down from the gates to the baths and the Westoe men were standing on the road outside the gates. So me and another lad walked up and addressed the Westoe men and we found out that they'd come down to the baths. The chairman of the lodge had been called over by the manager and asked to go with him to shift the Westoe men. The lodge official had got on to Durham and Durham also got on to him to move the Westoe men from the baths off NCB property.

> The lad I was with said to the pickets: 'Mind you're wasting your time with these lads, they won't come out with you.'

> But the pickets said: 'We don't want you to, we just want your support.' I said to meself after that: 'I disagree with this, my own chairman joining in with the Coal Board to shift men off NCB property.' I went to the lodge meeting and it was brought up that union officials should not join in with the colliery manager to move miners off NCB property. That's when I started to become active in the union.

Three Durham collieries, Dawdon, Easington and Westoe joined the strike for three days. The Yorkshire men were out for a fortnight and while they were out the NCB agreed to the full wage demand that had been submitted by the NUM to the Board in 1968.

Although this strike was short, it broke the spell that bound management and unions together and ended an era of co-operation. Not only had three lodges defied the NCB, they had also defied the moderate union leaders at Red Hill.

In 1970 the NUM demanded a wage increase of 33 per cent. The newly-elected Conservative government, under the leadership of Edward Heath, set a 12-per-cent limit on the wages of public sector workers. Left-wing coalfields campaigned for strike action if their demands were not met. When the NCB offered only half the claim, one thousand angry miners lobbied the NUM executive meeting, which decided to ballot the members to see if they were in favour of a strike, and to recommend a 'yes' vote.

The strike ballot was won when 55 per cent of the membership voted for, but it failed to reach the 65 per cent required by the rules of the NUM to call a strike. The militancy of the British miners was increasing, but its growth was uneven. Wales had voted 82 per cent in favour, Scotland 77 per cent, Kent 67 per cent, and Yorkshire 62 per cent. Durham, Nottingham, Midlands and Derbyshire had, in line with their leaders, rejected the strike call.

In Durham support for strike action was more popular among faceworkers than the lower-paid. In November a wave of strikes swept through the coalfield as over 110,000 miners took action. Seven pits in Durham either stopped work or implemented a go-slow. But when the wage

Blackhall Lodge committee 1970s

settlement was put to the members, it was accepted by a two-thirds majority.

At the 1971 NUM annual conference, rule 43, which required a two-thirds majority, was amended to require only 55 per cent.

In an attempt to close the widening gap between face workers' pay and those of the other grades, conference submitted a wage claim of £5 for face workers, £9 for back-bye men, and £6 for surface workers. When the NCB responded with an offer of £1.80 for face workers and £1.75 for other classes of miners the executive ordered an overtime ban to start on 1 November and a ballot for strike action on 22 November. This time the strike ballot exceeded the new 55-per-cent threshold by 3.8 per cent. Durham miners voted 55 per cent in favour.

The union was demanding a 17-per-cent increase for face workers and a 47- and 44-per-cent increase for back-bye and surface workers. The government on the other hand had set an 8-per-cent maximum for wage increases. This time a confrontation was unavoidable. From midnight on 8 January 1972 all the pits in Britain were on strike.

After the first week the Durham lodges were organised into groups, each one taking responsibility for picketing power stations, coal stocks and consumers in the industrial areas. Alan Napier was an eighteen-year-old apprentice at Murton colliery. Although he had had the chance of two apprenticeships outside the coal industry, he had decided to follow his father down the pit. He remembers:

> I was only eighteen, but I knew what the strike was all about. My father told me what we could expect going on strike for the first time since 1926.

> The weather was freezing when we went picketing and I had three layers of clothing on as well as a pair of my mother's tights. I remember it was Ref Garsite from Easington colliery who was directing the picketing on Teeside. He sent us to Smith's Dock at Middlesbrough. Three buses from Murton went down on the late shift. There were numerous gates to the docks and when we got there each gate had been given to a different colliery and they were all set up with braziers and they had built little wooden huts. We were sent down on the dock-side and it was freezing. Within an hour we had a brazier up and running but we were open to all the elements and the wind was bleaching in off us. We stopped about three wagons and got a good response from the wagon drivers. We were getting frozen so we decided to build our own shed.

> Close by us was a terrace of about four derelict houses. My father and Sammy Robson who worked with my father up the yard seam were given the duty of going over to the houses and getting some old doors. It was all boarded up and it was about one o' clock in the morning. So we set about pulling some of the doors off. I saw me father having a kick at one of these doors, the next thing I saw was a light going on and here's a fella standing in his underpants asking me father what the hell he was trying to do.

> That was the funny side, but in the course of that strike I went from 18 to 50 in terms of experience. It was a historic battle.

The deputies' union NACODs did not support the strike as they had separate wage negotiations.

Gala 1970s

When deputies were assigned to do work normally done by NUM members the miners' lodges picketed them. George Maitland was a fitter at Murton colliery. He recalls:

It got very nasty. Men were calling the deputies awful names. Some deputies were climbing over the wall into the car park so they didn't have to pass men who were their work-mates. You could tell when there was an unpopular deputy coming by the mood of the men. They would say: 'Here's that bastard coming.' If it was someone they liked they would just let them walk through and maybe shout: 'All right, young'n!'

We actually had overmen picketing with us because, for some reason, at Murton when a deputy became an overman he joined COSA [Colliery Overmen and Salaried Staffs Association] which was part of the NUM. Mind, after the strike a lot of them went back into NACODs. It got really nasty and very bitter.

By the beginning of February the government was reeling. Coal stocks were running out and power cuts were about to seriously affect industry. On 8 February the government declared a State of Emergency and the next day Robert Carr met the NCB and the NUM and increased the offer to £3.50 for surface workers and £3.00 underground. When the NUM rejected the offer, Carr set up a Court of Inquiry, led by Lord Wilberforce, to examine the level of wages in the mining industry. The NUM agreed to co-operate with the inquiry but not to be bound by its findings.

The picketing of coal depots continued. At Saltley coke depot, 100,000 tons of domestic coke had been stockpiled and the gas board refused to agree to a system where coke was distributed to hospitals and old people on the permit system, as operated at other depots. On 10 February, 44,000 Midlands car workers and engineers struck work in sympathy with the miners and marched on the depot. The police were heavily outnumbered and the chief constable ordered the gas board to close the depot. The management reluctantly agreed to operate a permit system. This was the defining moment in the 1972 strike which sent shock waves through the Establishment.

The Wilberforce Inquiry began its business in public on 15 February, when 1.2 million workers were laid off and twelve power stations had run out of coal. Within three days the inquiry concluded that miners' earnings were below those of other industrial workers and miners should therefore be treated as a special case. It recommended a £4.50 increase for face workers, £6.00 for back-bye men and £5.00 for surface workers.

The NUM executive rejected this offer by 13 votes to 12 but agreed to further negotiations. At 1.20 am Saturday 19 February they agreed to an improved offer giving all miners an extra seven rest days. When this new offer was put to the miners five days later, it was overwhelmingly accepted.

On 28 February production was resumed by miners who had won the first national strike. The Durham men had the added bonus that they had achieved parity with other coalfields. For the first time miners were united by the same pay structure and the same rates of pay.

The victory changed the union and changed relationships between men and management. Deputies were never again to hold the authority that they had enjoyed before the strike. As Jacky McCowliff confirmed:

> The animosity didn't end when we went back to work. There was absolute hell on. The lads

got stuck into shotfirers and deputies about what they had done. It simmered on for months with many bitter arguments.

The authority of the deputies had been undermined. We still worked alongside them and they could still give the men their jobs, but if they didn't get completed there was no recriminations, no more saying: 'Yer lazy bastards', no more of that. There was no more 'heeds down and arses up' with them. That ceased from day one going back.

A new-found confidence now prevailed and the NCB realised that it could no longer rely on a compliant NUM. In 1973 the executive committee recommended strike action but failed to convince the men, only 36 per cent voting for a strike.

Although the left did not have a majority on the national executive, their influence was growing. The right wing clung on to power with the narrowest of margins. One of their most prominent leaders was Tom Bartle of the Durham Colliery Mechanics Association. Despite being a national

executive member, he spoke out in 1973 in public against the recommendation of the committee to strike, which could not but influence many miners.

In July 1973 the NUM conference called for £45, £40, and £35 for face, back-bye and surface workers respectively. In October, in line with Phase Three of the government's pay policy, the NCB offered 7 per cent, which was rejected.

Miners picketing Satley coke depot

On 8 November the NUM called an overtime ban to start on Monday 12 November. Edward Heath was boxed into a corner. To give in to the miners' demands would have blown a huge hole in his wages policy. Coal stocks were still not high and a protracted strike would bring the country to a halt. To add to his misery, the Middle East oil-producing countries were restricting the flow of oil on to the markets and oil prices were rocketing. To use oil instead of coal in power stations was out of the question.

Heath did not wait for a strike ballot and immediately declared a State of Emergency. By 14 December all negotiations to find a solution had failed and Heath broadcast to the nation announcing a three-day week for industry to conserve coal stocks.

Throughout December and January all attempts by the government, NCB, TUC and NUM failed to reach a settlement and on 24 January a special delegate conference of the NUM decided to recommend a strike ballot to be held on 31 January.

This time it seemed that the whole union had united in the pursuit of a single goal. Even the moderate leaders campaigned for a 'yes' vote. Walter Malt, the general secretary of the Durham area NUM, toured the coalfield on 31 January urging miners to vote yes and even appeared on television news declaring: 'The lasses at Plesseys are earning more than a powerloader.'

When the result of the ballot was declared on 4 February it revealed that 80.99 per cent of the members had voted for a strike. This time Durham exceeded the national average, voting 85.70 per cent for action. On 7 February, two days before the strike was due to begin, Heath declared that the strike was not an industrial matter between employer and employee but a question of who ruled the country, the government or the unions. To decide the matter a general election was called for 28 February.

The deputies' union refused to cross picket lines and all was quiet at the pit gates. Picketing of coal-stocks never achieved the same scale as 1972 and the mining communities waited for the outcome of the election. After the votes were counted the Labour Party emerged with the greatest number of seats: 301, only five more than the Tories. Holding the balance of power were the Liberals with 14 seats.

Heath did not concede defeat immediately. For three days he attempted to form a coalition government with the Liberals. Only when he failed to persuade Jeremy Thorpe to join him did he relinquish power and give way to Harold Wilson. Michael Foot, who for so long had graced the platform of the Durham Big Meeting, was appointed Minister for Employment. Wilson granted the miners the full claim, including a payment for unsociable hours and £30 in lieu of an extra week's holiday. A further week's holiday was agreed for future years.

This was the single largest advance in earnings that the union had ever won and the miners' claim had triggered a course of events which effectively brought down the Heath government, an action for which they were never forgiven.

The oil price rises seemed to herald a great new future for coal and the Labour government devised a new Plan for Coal which anticipated that the country would require 150 million tons of coal per year by 1985. The Plan for Coal gave the miners grounds for optimism and on 14 March 1974 Derek Ezra visited Durham to announce a £5 million investment in Easington colliery to develop the under-sea reserves. But behind the scenes the NCB were laying plans to emasculate the NUM. NCB director Wilfred Miron drew up a battle plan to undermine the union's new-found unity. Central to this plan was the introduction of a bonus scheme.

The NUM had resisted any incentive schemes on the grounds that they were divisive and dangerous. In the opinion of many miners, to revert to the old system of paying men by the

amount of coal they produced could only encourage unsafe working practices. However, NUM president Joe Gormley was an enthusiastic supporter of such schemes, as were most of the moderate union leaders. In 1974 proposals to introduce an incentive scheme was rejected by the national conference and by a ballot, when 61 per cent of the membership voted against the scheme. A similar proposal was rejected by conference in 1977. Still not satisfied, the moderates insisted on a ballot, which was strongly opposed by the left wing but the right won the argument on the national executive committee and a ballot was organised.

The Kent area then applied to the Appeal Court for an injunction to stop the ballot on the grounds that it was unconstitutional since the incentive scheme had been rejected by the NUM national conference. Lord Denning ruled that 'the conference might not have spoken with the true voice of all the members, and in his view a ballot was a reasonable and democratic proposal'. The ballot was organised and the membership rejected the scheme by a majority of 55.75 per cent.

Despite the two ballots, the Nottinghamshire and South Derbyshire areas decided to ignore the rejection and negotiated Area Incentive Bonus Schemes. In doing this they were given full support and encouragement by Joe Gormley and the moderates on the executive.

Taking into account Denning's ruling, Yorkshire, South Wales and Kent sought an injunction to stop the incentive payment agreements. This time the judge was Mr Justice Watkins who made the following ruling: 'The result of a ballot nationally conducted is not binding upon the national executive in using its powers in between conferences.'

According to Denning, a union conference cannot reject an incentive scheme because it may not be reflecting the 'authentic voice of the members'. They should have a ballot because that is a 'democratic proposal'.

According to Watkins, the national executive committee *can* ignore the 'authentic voice of the members' even though they have expressed that voice in two ballots.

Once the incentive scheme was introduced in Nottingham and popular newspapers were broadcasting the increased earnings enjoyed by miners in this county, it was not long before every coalfield was operating the scheme.

In Durham a group of young miners were so disgusted at the way the incentive scheme had been introduced that they determined to organise a left movement and to change the moderate leaders. The Durham Left was formed that year. These young miners began to visit clubs in other villages on Friday nights to find other miners who agreed with them. They also started to attend the education schools run by the union where they met like-minded miners.

Typical of the young miners involved in the

Durham Left was David Hopper who became involved in the NUM lodge at Wearmouth colliery after the 1972 and 1974 strikes. There were a serious of disputes at Wearmouth over manning levels: the lodge insisted that places of work should be fully manned, whereas the NCB was prepared to run several faces at a time below the agreed manning level. These disputes led to a series of walk-outs in which Dave was involved.

He explained that one of the main grievances was the way the Durham executive was elected. He explained: 'The pits in Durham were split up into groups, each group having the right to elect one executive member. The system was being abused by lodge secretaries being in touch with each other and agreeing all to support a particular candidate, preventing the other lodges electing a member of their lodge.' By establishing contacts throughout

Miners lobby against incentive scheme

the coalfield the Durham Left were successful in getting a rule-change passed whereby each lodge had a turn in electing a member to the executive. This prevented left-wing lodges being blackballed by secret agreements. Wearmouth, Easington, Blackhall, and Hylton quickly established a reputation as militant lodges.

When Hylton colliery was threatened with closure in 1979 the men were prepared to fight to keep the colliery open and even volunteered to return to hand-filling to overcome the geological problems at the colliery. The Durham leadership was reluctant to make waves and were incensed when the left invited Arthur Scargill, then President of the Yorkshire area, to address a meeting in Southwick against the closure of Hylton colliery.

Dave Hopper remembered that the meeting was well attended, but:

> After the meeting we got taken in front of the executive committee and we had to explain our actions. But I think it did us more good than harm because a lot of miners thought: 'All the lads are doing is trying to save jobs, not trying to be undemocratic. They are just trying to get this issue discussed. The men at the pit want to fight but the Durham leadership doesn't want to fight.' I think that was one of the biggest boosts we had in trying to build up a caucus of left-wing thinkers.

The work of the Durham Left was to have a major

David Hopper

influence before the 1984 strike when Billy Stobbs from Easington was elected as the only rank-and-file miner to represent the Durham area on the national executive committee, swinging the balance of power to the left.

In 1978 the Labour government lurched from one crisis to the next and the Tories were busy preparing for office. The miners were at the top of the Tories' agenda. They drew up a strategy for taking on the miners which became known as the Ridley Report after its author, Nicholas Ridley.

His report had six principle aims:

1. Build up coal stocks

2. Make plans for the import of coal

3. Encourage non-union lorry drivers who would carry coal across picket lines

4. Introduce dual coal/oil-fired power stations as quickly as possible

5. Cut off welfare payments to strikers

6. Create a large, mobile squad of police to deal with pickets

In May 1979 they were elected into office and Margaret Thatcher became the first woman Prime Minister in Britain.

By 1980 a world slump was seriously undermining the strength of the NUM. Large quantities of cheap coal were flooding world markets. The rundown of the steel industry and heavy engineering caused a further collapse in the demand for British coal. Prices were falling rapidly and coal stocks were building up. It was estimated that 40 million tons of British coal was stock-piled at power stations when in February 1981 Derek Ezra, chairman of the NCB, announced that twenty-three pits were to be closed. In Durham Sacriston, Bearpark, Houghton and Boldon were to go immediately. A spontaneous strike wave broke out, spreading through the coalfields. South Wales, Kent, Midlands, Yorkshire and Scotland were all

Last shift, Boldon colliery 1982
Photo: Sunderland Echo

affected, including the four threatened pits in Durham. It looked as if a national strike was inevitable.

When the executive proposed a national ballot, Thatcher lost her nerve. The closure programme was shelved and a subsidy was granted to the industry to overcome its immediate problems. For many in the NUM this was a victory but some thought back to Red Friday 1925 when Baldwin's government bought time to prepare for the 1926 dispute.

In 1982 Arthur Scargill, the accepted leader of the left, was elected President of the NUM. His election campaign had been fought on a programme of opposing pit closures and advancing miners' wages. As if to deliberately inflame the situation, in September 1983 the government appointed Ian MacGregor, a 71 year-old 'union buster' from the USA, to be chairman of the NCB. On his appointment the NUM newspaper *The Miner* carried the headline: 'The Butcher Cometh'. No one now was in any doubt that the Tories were planning a confrontation.

In Durham the list of closures was growing. Hylton had closed in 1979, Blackhall and Houghton in 1981, Boldon in 1982 and East Hetton in 1983. All coalfields suffered a similar reduction in capacity. The situation resembled 1960 but with one obvious difference: in the 1960s there were some jobs to go to. Now there were practically none.

Miners in the Easington area, whose pits were long considered safe from closure, began to realise that they too could be vulnerable. The lodges joined with other organisations in the community to form the Save Easington Area Mines (SEAM)

campaign, which called a demonstration in Easington on 26 February 1984 and invited Neil Kinnock, the leader of the Labour Party, as the main speaker. The demonstration was led by the banner of Polmaise colliery in Scotland, which had been on strike for a week after the NCB had announced closure of the colliery.

On 1 March MacGregor announced the closure of Cortonwood colliery in Yorkshire. In response the Cortonwood miners resorted to strike action and by 6 March the whole Yorkshire Area was on strike. The action spread to Durham and on 9 March a special coalfield conference of the DMA called all Durham pits to take strike action against the threat of pit closures, pending a national ballot. By 14 March all Durham pits were idle.

Many reservations were voiced in the first weeks of the strike but Durham, true to its tradition of solidarity, held firm. Many miners may have suspected that the issues involved in the strike were profound and would not be easily resolved, but no one could have been prepared for what was to follow.

The majority of miners in Nottingham, South Derbyshire and Leicestershire refused to join the strike. The leaders of the dissident areas defended this action on the grounds that the national executive of the NUM had not called a national ballot. The question of the ballot came to dominate the debate both within and without the national union.

The tradition of calling national ballots was deep-rooted in the NUM and its predecessor, the MFGB. Despite the intentions expressed at its founding conference to create a single national union to integrate all area unions, the NUM remained a federation of autonomous trade unions. While these unions had the constitutional power to call area strikes without a ballot, a national strike required a national ballot.

David Guy was the treasurer of the Dawdon lodge and strongly in favour of striking to defend jobs. In the first days of the strike he remembered a fierce struggle in his lodge over the question of the ballot: 'The lads felt that it was their right to have a ballot and they didn't want this right taken off them. On the other hand, you had the younger men saying that the older men would just vote for redundancy. It was never a debate about the issues. Everyone agreed that the issue was right. Once the men

Seaham colliery   *Photo: Sunderland Echo*

realised that the rest of the coalfield was out, the ballot ceased to be an issue, it was just a question of getting behind the strike and winning as soon as possible.'

The debate at Dawdon was reflected nationally and the slogan, 'You're not going to vote me out of a job', became a prevalent argument.

Although many older miners were actively supporting the strike the younger men became the main force behind it and were the most active supporters of the 'no ballot' movement. They argued that a young man who would receive little in redundancy and had his working life before him was not voting for the same thing as an older man whose working life was at an end and would receive large redundancy payments. Since some pits were under immediate threat and others were considered safe, the miners at each individual pit should have the right to strike and not be denied that right by miners who considered that their jobs were safe.

Those against the ballot were quick to remind everyone that two national ballots had rejected the incentive scheme but these democratic ballots had been ignored by the areas now calling for a national ballot.

On 5 April thousands of miners, young and old, surrounded the NUM headquarters in Sheffield

David Guy

to lobby the executive calling on them not to hold a ballot. When an executive spokesman announced that they had decided not to call a ballot there were scenes of ecstatic cheering.

An even bigger lobby of 6,000 greeted the delegate conference on 19 April. This conference changed the rules on national ballots so that only a simple majority was required to call a national strike. However, the delegate conference rejected a call for a national ballot, and issued a statement calling on all miners to join the fight against closures.

After the conference had concluded its business,

hundreds of Durham miners who had been lobbying the conference retired to the Sheffield Labour club. When they tried to leave the club they found themselves surrounded by hundreds of South Yorkshire police who attacked the first men who came out of the club. Billy Stobbs, the president of Easington Miners' Lodge and Durham national executive member, was badly injured. Over twenty men were arrested.

In Durham the women in the SEAM campaign began to organise kitchens in the Easington area and soon, throughout the county, over 50 miners' support groups were formed to provide food for the mining communities. Durham remained totally solid for the first five months of the strike and many miners were sent to other areas to

Young miners cheer when NEC announces there is to be no ballot

Lobby of delegate conference 19 June 1984

picket. Hundreds of Durham miners were at Orgreave coking plant near Sheffield when 8,000 police, many on horseback, others in full riot gear, charged thousands of pickets. Over one hundred pickets were injured. Many were arrested and later charged with conspiracy, but were cleared at their trial after it was revealed that the BBC had doctored news footage to show that the police had charged only in response to stone throwing by pickets. In fact, mounted police had charged into the miners continuously throughout the day.

Throughout the summer of 1984 the NCB tried to persuade Durham's miners to return to work but to no avail. They calculated that if they could get some men back, at one or two pits, this would undermine the resolve of the strike.

Where miners were concentrated communities

around working pits, the authority of the union remained strong and the communal activity and support kept up spirits. In the villages in the west of the county, travelling miners were isolated and, despite the good work of the miners' support groups, less help was available in these areas. It was not surprising that the NCB concentrated its effort on these isolated men in a bid to get them back to work. On 20 August small group from the colliery officials' union COSA was taken into Wearmouth colliery and on the Friday of the same week a traveller from a west-Durham village was sneaked in the back of Easington colliery, which provoked a riot. The village of Easington was sealed off for a week and no one who looked like a miner was allowed to enter.

Police lines at Orgreave

Up to this point Durham had been policed mainly by the local constabularies. Now the county was flooded with police from Leicestershire, London and even Wales. Villages were in a state of siege as more and more miners were encouraged to break ranks and return to work. All through the winter the bitter struggle continued. Efforts to reach a settlement at national level came to nothing and, despite the valuable assistance channelled into the area from the rest of Britain and

Mounted police charge at pickets at Orgreave

Picketing at Easington

abroad, hardship was increasing day by day. By the last week of February 1985, the NCB estimated that 50 per cent of British miners were back at work.

On Sunday 3 March an NUM delegate conference passed a resolution calling for a return to work without an agreement. Throughout Durham miners marched proudly with their bands and banners back into the pit-yards. The honour of carrying the lodge banner was given to the women in recognition of their

Above: Billy Stobbs, in foreground, waits with pickets for solitary strikebreaker to arrive 25 August 1984

Photos: Keith Pattison

Right: After being assured by Easington colliery manager that strikebreakers would have to walk unaided through the main gate Easington miners erect barricade

Police occupy Easington colliery   Photo: Keith Pattison

strike, the NUM did not crumble under this pressure. At Westoe, Dawdon, Eppleton and Murton the union took strike action within months in defence of its members.

Dave Guy returned with his men at Dawdon which, despite its early reservations, proved to be one of the most solid pits. Only 133 had returned out of a labour force of 1,800.

magnificent efforts keeping families fed during the biggest and longest national strike of miners. At its end 60 miners were in jail, 700 had been sacked for minor offences during the strike, and thousands had suffered injuries as a result of police action.

Now the NCB was determined to demonstrate that they were in charge. At many pits the eight o'clock maintenance shifts were abolished and replaced by five o'clock shifts, a measure whose only justification could be to demoralise men. However difficult the circumstances resulting from a workforce having its ranks fractured during the

When we returned at Dawdon we marched into the pit-yard and turned round and marched out again as a gesture of defiance. Just to show the manager that the NUM still had an influence at the pit. I was at a low ebb. I was both mentally and physically exhausted.

Within three or four weeks we were out on strike. When that pit came out again solid I was back to normal. We had a big meeting and the problem with the manager was resolved. It showed that the resolve and determination was still there and that was the last thing that the management wanted.

On 6 June 1985 the coalfield was in mourning after the death of DMA treasurer Jimmy Inskip

Right: Confrontation
Easington   August 1984

Left: Easington under siege

and in the autumn the president of the DMA, Harold Mitchell, and the general secretary, Tom Callan, retired. David Hopper, the secretary of Wearmouth pit, was elected as general secretary and David Guy was elected president.

In the aftermath of the strike a seismic shift took place in the politics of different areas of the national union. The Nottingham delegates, with the exception of agents Ray Chadburn and Henry Richardson, walked out of the July conference of

Winter sets in January 1985   Photo: Keith Pattison

the NUM and later formed the Union of Democratic Miners (UDM). Several thousand miners in Nottingham, many of whom had been on strike throughout 1984-5, remained in the NUM and supported the left in the union. The Wales and Scottish Areas, who had traditionally been on the left of the union, moved to the right. The DMA, led now by left-wing agents, moved to the left, as did the Durham Mechanics who dominated Group 1. Before the strike, Bill

Miners' children queue for food

Photos: Keith Pattison

*Voting to return to work
Easington March 1889*

Etherington, the Dawdon Mechanics delegate, had been elected to replace Tom Bartle, the general secretary of the DCMA, who was killed in a car accident in London. Bill Etherington, who had been the secretary of the Dawdon Mechanics for many years, built up a reputation as a militant on the left within what was regarded as a moderate right-wing association.

In Durham the UDM were able to get a foothold only at Tursdale workshops and, to a lesser extent, at Wearmouth colliery. Most of these recruits were dissident mechanics, many of whom had been expelled from the DCMA during the strike for strike-breaking.

While in most areas the NUM was the recognised union, in Nottingham the NCB recognised only the UDM. Those miners who remained loyal to the NUM were not represented at colliery and area level: the Nottinghamshire NUM was banned from functioning as a union on NCB property.

Dawdon women campaign for release of jailed miners

After the strike the NCB announced the closure of 24 pits and 12 workshops, with the loss of 24,000 jobs. In the run-up to privatisation the NCB changed its name to British Coal.

Immediately after the strike Sacriston colliery was closed on the grounds of unsafe working conditions. Herrington colliery closed when the men voted not to go through the review procedure.

When it was announced in June that Horden colliery would close, the men took the colliery through the new Modified Colliery Review Procedure which had been agreed between NACODs and the NCB. Stewart Shields, the judge who presided over the final review, ruled that it was reasonable to close the pit as the social consequences and the social cost of closure were not a concern of British Coal.

Seaham colliery was closed after a review in the same year.

In December 1988 British Coal announced that at Dawdon colliery there were no workable reserves left in the E90 area of the pit. The proposed development in G80 and G81 was below a huge pond of water that had been discovered, containing an estimated 11 million gallons of water. In the interests of safety, management announced that they were to abandon 1 million

Photo: Keith Pattison

Geoff Hartnell holding poster, calling for his and other sacked miners' reinstatement. Geoff was sacked at Tursdale workshops after a complaint from the UDM. Although he won his Industrial Tribunal British Coal refused to reinstate him. Murton colliery was called out first in a series of one day strikes to reinstate the sacked men.

Billy Etherington, right, receives cheque for sacked miners from Ian Lavery Secretary of NUM Northumberland Area
Photo: Stan Gamester

tons of coal in this area. A plan to work the 3.8 million tons of reserves in C seam at the rate of 4,000 tons of coal per day and employing 1,000 men for four years was reluctantly accepted by the men. In the event, thinning of the C seam shortened this prediction and the colliery closed in July 1991. In October it was announced that Murton colliery was to be closed. All unions at the pit united to oppose the closure and miners were dissuaded from volunteering for redundancy or seeking transferral and to proceed through the review procedure. British Coal's tactics now changed as they became more impatient to speed up the rate of closures. To avert the delay of the review procedure they offered the miners what amounted to maximum payments of redundancy throughout the pit. After the experience of the Hordon, Seaham and, in particular, the Bates colliery review in Northumberland, the men voted to take the maximum payment and the pit closed in December.

When in October 1992 Heseltine announced that 32 collieries throughout Britain would close and that the Modified Colliery Review Procedure was to be suspended, there were only four pits left in Durham: Westoe, Wearmouth, Vane Tempest and Easington. All were on the closure list except Wearmouth, which was to be moth-balled pending its sale.

A wave of opposition such as had never been seen before in Britain swept through the country, but to no avail.

In October 1994 the winding towers of Wearmouth colliery were blown up, bringing to an end mining in Durham.

That year the Durham Miners Gala drew larger

Demolition of Wearmouth colliery winding towers
Photo: Sunderland Echo

crowds than had been seen for 30 years. In the Gala brochure the editor wrote:

The coalfield that was murdered

As we prepare to publish this brochure for the 110th Miners' Gala, the last deep mine in the county, Wearmouth colliery, is about to close. The hope that private capital would rescue the mine has faded and so an industry that has survived in this county for over 600 years has finally been destroyed by the short-term madness of an incompetent and revengeful government.

Over the centuries the miners of County Durham have earned vast wealth for the rich and powerful. Our miners fuelled the fires of the industrial revolution, bunkered the trading fleets for British commerce and heated the homes of the people.

But for the men who delivered this rich bounty the rewards were sparse and the price was often a tragic one for their wives and children. It has been estimated that the callous disregard for safety and the greedy quest for profit cost the lives of 100,000 British miners before the turn of the century.

To survive our communities had to stick together. They had to share what little they had, and they had to develop a sense of humour to relieve the hardships of the mine. Above all they had to band together into a union.

It is now two hundred years since the miners of Durham began their long and tortured struggle to combine together into a fighting force and escape from slavery.

It took almost a century of strikes, lockouts, evictions, military repression, shootings and hanging before the first stable union was established in 1869. From that time on the Durham Miners' Association was the only defence the mining communities of Durham had against injustice, disaster and, in times of lock-outs and depressions, even starvation.

The mining unions of Durham provided a welfare state long before Beveridge made his celebrated report. They provided homes for the old, education for the young, clinics for the villages and recreational facilities without rival

Wednesday 21 October 1992 London demonstration against pit closures
Photo: Stan Gamester

amongst the industrial working class.

Out of this struggle for a better future developed the concept that the mines should be nationalised. This was not just the miners' view. It was widely accepted at the start of the First World War that the old owners had brought the industry to its knees. For this reason the government of 1914 was forced to bring the mines under state control in order to produce enough energy for their war effort.

Later in 1919 the Sankey Commission reviewed the industry and later concluded that the Mines must be nationalised. Even the independent representatives of capital who sat on the committee agreed that it was in their interests. It was not however until the chaos of the Second World War and the election of a Labour government in 1944 that the idea was made into a reality on Vesting Day 1947. On that day miners stood proudly with their families in the pit yard and read the notice proclaiming: 'This Colliery is now managed by the NCB for and on behalf of the people'

Now miners were encouraged to increase their effort and pull the country out of the post-war fuel crisis. Promises were made. Nationalisation,

Vane Tempest campaign against pit closures October 1992
Photo: John Garrett

miners were told, would prevent the closure of mines by allowing the profitable mines to subsidise those with higher production costs. Nearly four decades later, in 1984, the sons and grandsons of those miners who had stood, full of hope, in the pit yard on Vesting Day were locked in a deadly conflict with the government for the very survival of the industry.

The NUM had warned that the intention of the Tory government was to destroy the industry and with it the miners' union and our communities. We were derided as alarmists.

For a whole year the miners of County Durham were locked in battle with the NCB and a nationally organised police force. It seems now unbelievable that the mining villages of Durham could have endured the hardships of that year but the old traditions of the past had not died. The communities pulled together.

In answer to Thatcher, a massive women's movement formed, with over 50 separate branches in the county collecting food and serving it to the families in vast kitchens. We now know that many members of the public were not familiar with our history and did not fully appreciate our concerns and could not understand what all the fuss was about. Some were taken in by a hostile press that condemned the miners as violent.

For them there is the excuse that they did not know. For others there is no excuse. The TUC leadership failed the miners at a time when a blow could have been struck at the Thatcher government that would have saved the British people some of the damage they were to enure in the subsequent years.

As for the leaders of the Nottinghamshire and the South Derbyshire miners, history itself has written their epitaph.

The aftermath of the strike was, if anything , harder to endure than the strike itself. Although the techniques of mining had progressed from the last century the tactics of management remained rooted in the past. Hundreds of men in the county were sacked for their part in the strike, dozens were imprisoned.

If, however, the intention of Thatcher was to destroy the National Union of Mineworkers and what it represents, she was to prove less enduring than the miners' union. She was unceremoniously removed from office by her own party members.

It was the rash overconfidence of her main opponent in the Conservative Party, Heseltine, that, in 1992, brought the miners back on to the agenda. This time the people responded. They understood the arguments and what was at stake. They responded in their tens of thousands. From the Georgian town houses of Cheltenham to the housing schemes of Glasgow the people of Britain came out on to the streets. On Wednesday 21 October 1992, over a quarter of a million people marched on the streets of London in support of the miners. The following Sunday, 25 October, saw an even bigger demonstration.

This was one of those rare moments in our history when the people awaited the call of leadership to support the miners in industrial action. There was no excuse this time. The whole country was hostile to the pit closures programme. Even the police seemed apologetic for their excesses of 1984.

Durham miners' president, David Guy, presenting Nelson Mandela with a memento at the conference of the National Union of Mineworkers of South Africa

A delegation of South African miners spent three weeks as guests of the North East Area NUM in 1990
Back l to r: A Marghum, D Temple, G Hopper, F Mahlango, G Jackson, J Cogdon, E Ramaila
Front row, l to r: A Nugent, G Nkadimeg, Coun. Mrs E Tully, Coun. J McCormack, S Mamekoa,   Coun. GDH Cole, J Presley, W. Etherington

Crowds listening to speeches, Gala 2000

But the call never came; the TUC leadership stayed true to its history and for the third time this century, betrayed the miners. The moment passed, the people began to grow weary of just marching.

The TUC advised the miners to leave the fight to the Parliamentary Labour Party and their representatives on the Trade and Industry Select Committee. A crumb was offered and not for the first time, these representatives gratefully accepted. The stay of execution that was offered, in the absence of a real fight, became an execution. To date more pits have closed than were on the original list.

We mentioned earlier the sense of humour that has helped the Durham miner through many hard times. But keen as this humour is it cannot diminish the resentment and bitterness we feel against all those who over the years sucked the lifeblood from our county and then when it was convenient for them, abandoned its people in the industrial desert that they created.

In the year 2000 the Durham Area NUM, continues to fight for all those thousands of miners who are still suffering the effects of working in the mining industry and to have the full pensions restored to those who were sacked in the 1984 dispute. The Durham Miners Gala, that celebration of our rich heritage of struggle continues to flourish. In the last Gala brochure of the twentieth century this tribute was paid to the Durham spirt:

The Durham spirit marches on

The Durham Miners' Gala is safe for the New Millennium.

This is the verdict of the people of Durham and our many friends throughout the trade union movement who have rallied to save this precious institution. There were those who thought that the Big Meeting had no relevance once Durham deep mines had been destroyed, but they have been proved wrong. By raising the finance to continue the Gala the communities have demonstrated that our Day in Durham means more than just mines. The Durham Miners Gala is not so much about the hewing of coal as the hewing of a society

It was of course the exploitation of coal in Durham that gave rise to Durham communities. But it was the exploitation of the miners and their families which gave rise to a community spirit much more precious and lasting than the coal.

This spirit formed the first trade unions, the first death and accident funds, libraries and schools, welfare organisations, co-operative stores, clubs, Brass Bands, football and athletic clubs, all founded, administered and financed by working men and women. In the face of adversity Durham people constructed their own compassionate society.

This spirit of mutual dependence sustained us in the darkest hours when the selfish pursuit of profit maimed and destroyed thousands of miners and blighted their families. Lock-outs and strikes, which established our right to justice, could only be endured by a collective responsibility for the welfare of the individual. It is a spirit which has proclaimed that ultimately the future depends upon ourselves. This is as true and as necessary today as it ever was.

The decades of neglect and then the final destruction of the mining industry have created many problems. Unemployment and low pay has left their mark on three generations. Drugs abuse, once only associated with inner city deprivation, has invaded our villages. Depopulation leads to empty housing stock, the target of slum landlords. All these problems have to be addressed and to address them we need our history. We need that spirit and those values with which our forefathers fought for a freedom, justice and a better life.

Many of our banners have faded and decayed, as banners made of cotton or silk do in the course of time, but in the face of new problems new banners are being made, in more and more communities. Banners are not cheap but committees have been set up, old comrades have rallied to raise thousands of pounds to ensure that this Gala will see again banners once laid to rest when the mine closed. More will follow next year.

This activity is not pure nostalgia harking back to a bygone age but a living movement; testimony to the unfailing spirit that makes the Durham Miners Gala a force for the new Millennium

Sponsors of the
Durham Miners' Millennium Book

Adamson B
Adamson James
Addison John George
Adey DA
Ainscough Walter
Alexander David
Allen Mrs Darlene
Allen Keith
Allerdyce Mr.S
Allison Arnold
Allison John J
Anderson B
Anderson Mr. M.
Anderson Thomas Windship
Anderson William
Appleby James H
Argent Mr D
Armstrong L
Armstrong T W
Armstrong Mr & Mrs
Aspinall Peter
Aspinall Rita
Atkinson Brendan Thomas
Atkinson Graeme
Atkinson H
Atkinson Marjorie and Rita,
    Atkinson "The Twins"
Atkinson Mr A
Atkinson Mr R C
Atkinson Mr
Atkinson Mrs A
Atkinson Peter

Atkinson Stephen
Austin L
Austin Mrs B
Austin Barry
Austin Bid
Aylesbury Eric
Aylesbury Thomas
Ayre R
Bainbridge Arthur
Bainbridge Mr G
Baines P R
Baker AG
Baker I
Baker John
Baker Mr J
Bales M
Ball Jim
Balfour Alec
Banfold J R
Barker Gerald
Barker Mr
Barrett Mr G
Barrow Craig Stuart
Barrow Janice
Barry C
Bate Jewel
Batey Paul
Batty Mr T
Beadle J H
Beckwith Mrs Jean
Bedford Mr & Mrs
Bedford Ms

Bell D
Bell Mr J
Bell Mr J E
Bell Pat
Bell Stan
Belshaw David
Belshaw W
Bennett Mrs I
Benney Steve
Bentham Mr R N
Benfold J R
Bescoby W H
Besserman J
Bewley John
Bexley Jomo
Binnett M
Bird Joe
Black Raymond
Bland John
Boddy W
Boggan Mr M
Bond Mrs Ena
Bonell Mr H
Bowden W P
Bowker Andy
Bowmaker James
Bowman Philip
Box Edward J
Boyd T H
Branfoot Mr D W V
Breeze Mr M J
Brenkley A

Brennan Mrs M J
Brennan Paul and Paula
Brennan Mr James
Brewster Mr I
Briggs Ann
Brigham Magnus
Brotherstone Terry
Brown Jeffrey
Brown Neville
Brown Mr T H
Brown R
Brown Robert James
Brumler Catherine
Brumwell Mr W
Bryan Mr L
Buchanan Mandy
Buck B
Buckham Mrs A
Buckingham Mr S
Bull Jim
Burchell Graham
Burke Alexander
Burlinson Mr J E
Burlison G F
Burney G I
Burns Mrs M
Butler W G
Cairns J L
Cairns James W
Cairns John
Cairns Mrs M C
Cairns William
Cairns James W
Calvert Alan
Campbell J
Campbell W E
Carr J J
Carr Laurence
Carr Mr T E
Carty Mr John
Ceppleton John Smith
Chambers Barry
Chambers Colin G
Charlton Joseph
Charlton M

Charlton Mr R
Chatterton Mrs P
Chilley Mr F B
Chrisp Paul
Clair W
Clare Michael H
Clark George
Clark J A
Clark J M
Clark W J
Clarke Mr E J H
Clarke Mr W T
Claughan Mr L
Clews Mr Wilfred George
Clish Mr K
Clough Kenneth
Cogdon Mr Joe
Colman G S
Connor Brian
Connor B & E M
Connor C G
Connor H
Conway Mr G J
Cook John
Cook Mr George Rolan
Cook Mr A
Cook Mrs E
Corrigan J
Cotogno Mr A
Coulson J
Cowan Mr and Mrs J
Cowley E
Coyles Mr Stanley
Craddock Cllr. W
Craggs Andrew
Cram John
Crane G
Cranmer Mr R W
Crawford Mr M
Crayon Pete
Crossley K
Crozier T S
Cufflet G
Cummings Mr T
Curry Mr Norman

Dairies N B
Darwin B R
Daughtery G T
Davidson John
Davidson Mr R
Davis Mr A G
Davison Brian
Davison James
Davison John
Davison R
Dawe Maurice
Dawson Colin
Dawson Mr R
Dawson W
Day Alan
Day Thomas
Defty Mr J O
Deighton D
Dinning Harry
Ditchburn K
Dixon Eric G
Dixon Joseph W
Dodds Fred
Doddy Martin
Dodsworth Thomas
Donaghy Rita
Donaldson Mr J
Donnelly Thomas
Donnelly Sue
Douch Lucy
Douglas Ms Deborah
Doyle Sue and Peter
Dry Jim
Duffy S
Dukes D W
Dunn Betty
Dunn C K
Dunn Mr D
Dunn William
Dunning Richard T
Dyson R
Eastick T
Eavis Dorothy Ritson (Nee Now)
Ede J
Edwards Stanley

Eilbeck T
Elliot Joy
Elliott Mr A
Elliott Pete
Ellis Mr H.
Embleton R
Emery Norman
Emery Stanley
Emmerson John
Erskine Mr R
Ersline Linda
Evans Alfred
Evans D
Evans David
Evans G
Fail Jeffrey
Falconer Mr A
Fallow John
Fallow T
Fawcett William
Fergus Stephen
Ferguson Richard
Findlay Mr J
Fisher J D
Fisher Malcolm
Fitz-Gerald R J
Fleming Charles
Flynn Mr Wilf
Forbes Mr P
Forkin Mr Patrick
Fortune Keith
Foster J
Foster Mr R
Fox Mr T H
Freeman George
Freeman John
Frost Stanley
Frostwick W
Frow Ruth
Fulthorpe George
Garnham G
Garside Mr Ian
Gavin Mr T B
Geldart Mr R W

Gibson A
Gibson David
Gibson R
Gilbert M
Gilbert Miriam (Nee Atkinson)
Gittins J G
Gladwyn L
Glass Marie
Glaughan Mr L
Glendenning Mr R
Gothard Michael
Goundry F L W
Graham Mr Robert W
Graham Mr D
Graham P
Grant Mrs M
Grassby Jack
Gray Barry & Valerie
Gray Miss W M
Greathead A
Green G R
Green Royston
Green Mr K
Green Ronald
Gregson Snr Ron
Gregson Jnr Ron
Griffiths Goeff
Guy John Edward
Hagen J
Haggan Arthur
Hall J G
Hall Mr Robert
Hall Mr M K
Hall Stephen
Halliday Trevor
Hamilton John
Hancock Mr T
Handy Ben
Hanley A E
Hardy Mr G
Harker J W
Harker Maurice
Harley Ron
Harper Dr. Jim E

Harper Mick
Harper Stanley
Harper William M
Harrison Silas
Hartley William
Hawker Glyn
Heath Mr S
Henderson Mr & Mrs D
Henderson Norman
Hendy QC John
Heslop Frank
Heslop Thomas
Hicks Mrs I
Hind Leslie
Higgins Colin J
Higgins J R
Higgins Mrs E V
Hildore Keith
Hilton Mr P
Hitch Mr W
Hitch Mrs C
Hobson Mr R
Hogg Mr Robert
Hogarth D T
Hold Mrs G
Holden Mr R
Holden R T
Holland M B E Lawrence
Hooper Mr Bob
Hooper Mr Robert Alistar
Hopper Garry
Hopper David
Hopper Timothy
Hope R
Hopkins Mr F
Hopps George
Hornsey Mr I
Horsfield Wm
Horsley Mrs K C
Howe Chris
Howe DS
Howe Ronald
Hubbard Elizabeth (Nee New)
Hughes Joe

Hughes Mr and Mrs
Hully Mr William
Hutchinson W C
Illingworth Mr I
Irwin Joseph
Jackson A
Jackson K
Jackson Kenneth
Jackson Mr A
Jacob C
Jarrett Mr G
Jeddon Mark
Jellis Lorna Mrs (Nee Nutter)
Jennings S
Jennings Stewart
Johnson E
Johnson H G
Johnson Mr Robert
Johnson Mrs K
Johnson Thomas
Johnstone Mr W
Jolly J
Jones Paul
Jones Steven
Kay Charles
Keegan Thomas
Kell D A
Kendal Mr Charles
Kennan Mrs Norma
Kennedy E
Killip R
King Mr J
Kirlew Mr Michael
Kitchin P
Kitching John R
Knaggs Mrs Helen
Knowles K
Knox A
Lackenby Matthew H
Lahiri Mrs E
Laidlaw R
Laidler Mr W
Lamb Mr Thomas
Lamb T C

Lamb Jacky
Lambert Herbert
Lambeth Mr R
Lambton John
Langelier Colin
Larssen Davis
Lawrence Liz
Laws Mr Thomas
Lawson B C
Leadbitter Janet
Leadbitter Mr and Mrs J
Leadbitter Mr N J
Lee Bob and Jill
Lee Harold
Lee Joseph
Lee J P
Leslie Mr A
Lewis Peter
Liddell Ken
Lidster Mr J E
Lightfoot Dorothy (Nee Atkinson)
Lilley Mr James Hann
Linnett Alan
Lloyd Merion
Lockyer Mr R M
Long R
Lowe John
Lowery D A
Lucking D A
Lumsdon John
Lynch Mr W J
Lyons Mr Ervin
MacPherson Myrtle
MacPherson G
Macveigh Joe
Madrell George William Terrans
March Brian
Marr Stan O
Marshall Mrs V
Martin William
Mason Frederick
Mason Stephen
Matchett Chris
Matthews Mr D W

Matthews T
Maughan Mr J E
McAdam W
McCormick Colin
McCourt J and L
McCowliff John
McDowell R A
McGuire J
McKay Fiona
McKenna Mr J
McKie Mr W
McLaren Mr P
McLaughlin Mrs E
McLaughline Mrs
McLean Mrs S L
McLoram Joseph
McNally J
McWilliams Jim
Meadows Phil
Meale Alan
Mearman Jimmy
Meek C
Metcalfe JW
Metcalfe Thomas
Middlemas P
Middleton E
Millar David
Miller J
Miller Thomas Fishwick
Miller Tommy & Suzanne
Miller Rosemary
Miller Emily Clare
Milligan Suzan
Mitchell Abie
Mole Mrs Elsie
Mole Peter
Monarch J A
Montgomery Mr J
Moody John
Moody John Thomas
Moody T
Moore A
Moore F C
Moore William

Morey Ms E
Morgan D
Morgan Michael
Morgan Mr J G
Moriarty G
Morris Henry
Morrison Mr D
Morson S
Mould Mr T
Mullen James
Mulligan J
Munro Mrs M
Murdoch David
Nairn George
Nattrass J G
Naunton Graham
Needham Mrs Maureen (Nee Nutter)
Nesbit A
New David John
New John
New Lisa
Newbury P R
Nichols Thomas
Nicholson Thomas
Nicholson Ray
Nixon Joseph Edward
Noble Mr G R
Nogarth D T
Nugent A
Oates Linda
Ogden Mr N S
Oldham Unison
O'Marr Mr S
Orchard D
Ormerod Mrs I
OSullivan C
O'Sullivan C
Ott Max E
Ovington R
Paisley S R
Park Thomas
Parker Tony
Parnaby G

Parnaby Leonard
Parry William
Parsons Harry
Patterson Mrs Annie
Peacock Mr G T
Peacock Mr and Mrs R
Pearson M N
Pearson Mr J T
Peat Joseph
Peters Nancy (Nee Ritson)
Phillipson William
Pinkney Graham Luke
Pinkney J
Pirani Simon
Pirt David
Porthouse Mr E J
Potter W F
Powell Joseph
Powell Richard
Powney Bill
Pratt L R
Pratt Mr George
Prest James
Pritchard Trevor
Punshon John
Purvis O S
Pye G E
Quigley Cll John
Quigley Malcolm & Catherine
Quinn A
Race Thomas William
Raine Dennis
Raison William
Ramshaw J E
Rand Mrs D A
Reay P
Redden Mr C
Reed Mr Joseph
Reed Robert H
Reid John
Remmer Kevin
Richardson Mr B
Richardson Richard
Ridley Christopher

Ridley David
Riley Mr I
Roberton Carol
Roberts E
Roberts R W
Robinson Clive
Robinson David
Robinson Ken
Robinson Thomas
Robinson W
Robson C
Robson George W
Robson J W
Robson Joe
Robson L
Robson Mr T
Robson Mr W
Robson R
Rochester Mrs E
Rose Bud
Roseberry J B
Routledge J G
Rowell Alan
Rowlings Mr D
Ruddock Ronald
Russell K E
Sabin Bruce
Saint Willim
Saltmarsh R
Sargeant M H
Sarginson James
Sanford MP, Phil
Scarth James
Scott Mrs D
Scott John
Scott Mr J
Scott Mr J W
Scott Mr Derrick
Seddon Mark
Shackler J B A
Shaw Ian John
Shepherd Mr B
Shiel Mr D
Simpson G

Sissons Ms Christine
Skelhorn Louise
Smirk Mr E V
Smith Colin
Smith D
Smith D W
Smith F
Smith G
Smith Mark P
Smith Mr Colin
Smith Mr Jim
Smith M
Smith Imelda
Smithson J T
Snaith Matthew W
Snell Philip D
Snell T M
Snowdon Richard
Soppitt John
Southern Mr E
Spark Stanley
Spence D M M
Sproston O
Spurrier T
Staines Mr Robert
Steel Mr J
Steel Mr John E
Stephenson Mrs V
Stephenson Norma
Stewart A
Stobbart John Shaw
Stoodley Miss M
Stothard Miss P L
Stowells Brian
Strickland Simon
Stuart Brian
Stubbs T W
Sugden Mr R
Summers Mr A
Surtees Mrs E
Swinhoes of Boldon Colliery
Syer
Sykes Mr F
Talbot Mr S F E
Talbot Paul

Tate Mr Robert
Tate P
Tatters J C
Taylor George
Taylor Warwick H
Teasdale Alan
Ternent Ken
Thirlwell N
Thomas D
Thomas Wright
Thompson Albert
Thompson D S
Thompson K
Thompson Mr J
Thompson Norman
Thompson William
Thomson W
Thwaites A
Todd Stanley
Tomlinson Mr J
Tough Mr E D
Turnbull J W
Turnbull James H
Turner Doris
Underwood Betty
Urwin C
Usher Brian S
Van Buiten S
Vardy Henry
Vardy Mr A
Varty Mr T
Vincent T
Vine Mrs M
Vowles Beryl
Walker Charles Alan
Walker Mrs A
Walker Norman
Walker William T
Waller Mr John R H
Waller Robert
Walters Martin
Walton Bill
Wanless Colin
Ward S
Watson D

Watson G
Watson George
Wears Harland
Welch R
Wells R
Westgarth Paul
Westgarth Geo F
Weston Paul
Whitfield Bill
Whitfield Brian
Wild Liz
Wilding C
Wilkinson D
Wilkinson Joseph
Wilkinson Mr George W
Wilkinson Mr W B
Wilks Anne
Williams A M
Williams D E
Williams Kevin
Williams Mr T
Williams Ned
Williams Robert W
Williams Tommy "Squire"
Williamson Mr N
Williamson Mrs L
Wilson Chris
Wilson Mick
Wilson Mr M
Winn Rowland
Winship Thomas
Winter Dennis
Witts Brian
Wood Malcolm
Wood S
Worthy J
Wray Robert F
Wright Mary
Wright Mr A R
Yarnell Tom
Young Roger and Lynne
Young W
Younger Mr Colin
Younger Paul

Organisations

ASLEF Hitchin Branch
Beamish Open Air Museum
Durham Aged Miners' Homes
Association
Durham County Libraries
NUM Durham Area
Embsay Steam Railway
Ferryhill Town Council
FBU Region 10

FBU Region 14
Spennymoor Town Council
T.U. Studies & Information Unit
UNISON City of Sunderland
UNISON East Ayrshire
UNISON Fife
UNISON Frenchay Branch
UNISON Hartlepool
UNISON Herefordshire

UNISON North Tyneside
UNISON Northgate Prudhoe
UNISON Oldham
UNISON South Gloucestershire
UNISON Southern Region
UNISON Southhampton District
UNISON Wearside Branch
UNISON Woolwich
UNISON Yorkhill Branch